Customer Satisfaction

WAVE

™

THOMSON LEARNING

ACSP-COR3-7101A
Revision 1.5

Trademarks

Contents

Introduction 1
   Training Program Overview 1
   Course Purpose 1
   Course Goals 2
   Scenario-Based Learning 2
   Multimedia Overview 3
      Videos 3
      Assessment 3

Chapter 1—Customer Service 5
   Objectives 6
   Pre-Test Questions 6
   Introduction 7
   The Customer 8
   Top Ten Service Expectations 9
   Customer Interaction Skills 11
   Summary 12
   Post-Test Questions 13

Chapter 2—The Customer Service Organization 15
   Objectives 16
   Pre-Test Questions 16
   Introduction 17
   Organizational Structure 18
      Telephone Help Desk 18
      Field Service Organization 19
      Depot Service 20
   Help Desk Challenges 20
      Balance Paperwork and Customer Urgency 20
      Establish a Structured Escalation Policy 21
      Review all Customer-Related Documentation 21
      Maintain an Orderly Work Area 22
      Respect all Copyright Limitations 22
   Summary 23
   Post-Test Questions 23

Chapter 3—DIReCtional Troubleshooting   25

Objectives 26
Pre-Test Questions 26
Introduction 27
Define the Problem 29
    Describe Your Customer's Problem 29
    Determine the Problem Type 31
    A Quick Fix 33
    Document Everything 34
    Set Expectations 35
Isolate the Problem 36
    Reproduce the Problem 36
    Classify the Problem 37
    Reconfirm the Problem with the Customer 37
    Document the Status 37
Resolve the Problem 38
    Research the Problem 38
    Identify Potential Causes and Eliminate the Improbable 41
    Solve the Problem 41
    Repeat/QC Solution 41
    Document the Resolution 42
Confirm the Resolution and Expectations 42
    Review Case History 42
    Confirm with the Customer 43
    Open Service Calls 43
Broadcast the Solution 44
Document the Final Findings 44
Summary 45
Post-Test Questions 46

Chapter 4—Communication Skills   47

Objectives 48
Pre-Test Questions 48
Introduction 49
Effective Listening Techniques 50
    Face-to-Face Techniques 50
    Telephone Techniques 52
Questioning Skills 53
    Open-Ended Questioning Techniques 53
    Close-Ended Questioning Techniques 54
    Comparing Open- and Close-Ended Questions 55
Handling Difficult Situations 56
    Be ALERT! 56

Setting Expectations...58
    Establish a Working Partnership with Your Customer 58
    Promise Only What You Can Deliver 59
    Set a Realistic Resolution Time Frame 59
    Document Commitments and Dates 59
Following Up...60
    Deliver on Commitments, Time Frames, and Solutions 61
    Ensure Your Customer's Complete and Total Satisfaction 62
    Solicit Suggestions for Services and Process Improvements 62
    Avoid Future Problems by Documenting Problem Resolutions......................62
    Update Customer Records for Future Service and Support Needs...................63
Compile Frequently Asked Questions 63
Summary 64
Post-Test Questions...64

Chapter 5—Customer Interaction Skills Case Scenarios   **67**

Objectives...68
Introduction 68
DIReCtional Troubleshooting Model..70
    Hardware, Software, and Environmental Conditions Checklist 71
Customer Interaction Skills Microcomputer Support Case Scenarios–Part One..............72
    The Situation...72
    The Calls 72
    Call One 73
    Call Two 75
    Call Three..76
    Call Four 78
    Call Five 80
Customer Interaction Skills Microcomputer Support Case Scenarios–Part Two 81
    The Situation...81
    The Calls 81
    Call One 82
    Call Two 84
    Call Three..85
    Call Four 87
Customer Interaction Skills Microcomputer Support Case Scenarios–Part Three 88
    The Situation...88
    The Calls 89
    Call One 90
    Call Two 91
    Call Three..92
    Call Four 94
    Call Five 96

Customer Interaction Skills LAN Support Case Scenarios 97
    The Situation 97
    The Calls 98
    Call One 99
    Call Two 101
    Call Three 103
    Call Four 105
    Call Five 107
Customer Interaction Skills Network Interface Card Case Scenarios 108
    The Situation 108
    The Calls 109
    Call One 110
    Call Two 112
    Call Three 114
Customer Interaction Skills Wide Area Network Support Case Scenarios 117
    The Situation 117
    The Calls 118
    The Caldecott Corporation Wide Area Network 118
    Call One 119
    Call Two 121
    Call Three 124
Customer Interaction Skills Internet Support Case Scenarios 127
    The Situation 127
    The Calls 128
    Call One 128
    Call Two 130
    Call Three 131
Customer Interaction Skills Macintosh Support Case Scenarios 133
    The Situation 133
    The Calls 133
    Call One 134
    Call Two 136
    Call Three 137
    Call Four 139

Appendix A—Answers to Pre-Test and Post-Test Questions   **141**

Appendix B—Case Scenarios   **145**

Index   **159**

Introduction

TRAINING PROGRAM OVERVIEW

This training program includes material for certification purposes and supplemental material for reference only. The material in this program is presented in various formats, including printed books, electronic books, and interactive multimedia. You can access the electronic books and interactive multimedia from the Interactive Learning CD-ROM by clicking on the appropriate button on the opening screen.

- Certification Material

  Click on this button to access material required for certification: Digital Videos, NEXTSims, and *Challenge! Interactive*. The information you access reinforces the material contained in two manuals: *A+ Core Hardware* and *A+ Operating Systems (OS)*.

- Supplemental Material

  Click on this button to access supplemental reference material: Digital Videos and NEXTSims. You should use this material for job performance preparation, not exam preparation. The information you access reinforces the material contained in three manuals: *Navigating DOS and Windows 3.x*, *Navigating Windows 95 and Windows NT Workstation 4.0*, and *Customer Satisfaction*.

COURSE PURPOSE

The role of the Computer Support Professional is vital in today's business environment. Organizations have invested millions of dollars in information technologies, but if the skills of people are not at a high level or if the systems do not work, then this investment will not be realized. Your role in keeping people and systems productive is essential.

This course is designed to help coach you through problem diagnosis and troubleshooting processes. Wave's DIReCtional Troubleshooting Model outlines a methodical series of deductive steps that can be applied across industry platforms. These skills are augmented by five essential professional communication skills that integrate into the model providing a total problem resolution approach.

The *Customer Satisfaction* course has been developed directly from the CompTIA A+ Certification objectives, the industry standard since 1993. Wave Technologies has been a leader in A+ Certification Training since the inception of this program. In addition to the core materials, there are programs on networking and the Internet, navigating Microsoft Operating Systems, Macintosh technologies, and customer interaction skills. Real-life situations, the ones you will deal with every day, will often involve more than one—sometimes even all—of these areas.

COURSE GOALS

During this self-study course, you will be provided with the information you need to complete the following:

- Describe the relationship between good computer support, customer expectations, and customer problems.
- Apply the Wave DIReCtional Model to Troubleshooting, thus ensuring a consistent and comprehensive approach to solving customer problems.
- Communicate effectively and efficiently with customers, whether they are down the hall or across an ocean.
- Successfully test your skills in detailed real-life scenarios.

SCENARIO-BASED LEARNING

This self-study manual uses a number of scenario-based learning exercises. In these, you are presented with a situation similar to those you are likely to encounter in day-to-day support and management. You will be provided with the information you need and asked to determine the best solution. A suggested solution is provided at the back of the self-study manual.

These exercises are being used to supplement hands-on practice and to help get you started thinking critically about practical applications. In some cases, they have been used as a replacement for hands-on practice for scenarios where it would be especially difficult to emulate a real-world situation.

It is important that you take the time to work through the scenario-based exercises. These are an important supplement to the training materials and are meant to reinforce the text information in your manual.

MULTIMEDIA OVERVIEW

The Interactive Learning CD-ROM is a robust collection of learning tools designed to enhance your understanding and prepare you for certification. Click on the appropriate button on the opening screen to access the available media.

Videos

A key element of the Interactive Learning CD-ROM included with this course is digital video. Digital video lessons describe key concepts covered in the manual. Often concepts are best understood by drawing a picture. Digital video segments provide a graphical illustration, accompanied by an instructor's narration. These lessons are ideal both as introductions to key concepts and for reinforcement.

Assessment

As reinforcement and review for certification exams, the *Challenge! Interactive* is significantly helpful. The *Challenge!* contains sample test items for each exam. The sample tests are comprised of multiple-choice, screen simulation, and scenario questions to better prepare you for exams. It is a good idea to take the *Challenge!* test on a particular exam, read the study guide and then take the *Challenge!* test again. It is useful to take the *Challenge!* tests as frequently as possible because they are such excellent reinforcement tools.

Customer Service

MAJOR TOPICS

Objectives 6

Pre-Test Questions... 6

Introduction 7

The Customer.. 8

Top Ten Service Expectations............................. 9

Customer Interaction Skills 11

Summary 12

Post-Test Questions 13

CHAPTER 1

OBJECTIVES

At the completion of this chapter, you will be able to:

- Outline the connections between good support and customer loyalty.
- List the most important customer expectations for support.
- Relate the various interdependent skill sets that comprise good computer support.

PRE-TEST QUESTIONS

The answers to these questions are in Appendix A at the end of this manual.

1. Why has the role of the computer support professional become a mission-critical position?

   ....

   ....

2. Why are customers a valuable business asset?

   ....

   ....

3. What are the three skills competencies required for a successful computer support professional?

   ....

   ....

INTRODUCTION

The role of the Computer Support professional is becoming mission critical in today's fast changing business and technical worlds. Organizations have invested millions of dollars in information systems; but the power of these technologies cannot be realized unless the systems are operational and the people are capable of making them work. Your role is to keep both your organization's systems and people productive. This is a vital job in terms of increased productivity and reduced costs. Management is very involved and interested in both of these dimensions.

Organizations are becoming very aware of the cost of "down time." When systems are not operational, thousands, if not millions, of dollars are lost. As businesses become more reliant on information technology, literally everything can succeed or fail based on the viability of the computer system. The people skills and support data are harder to verify, but these also have a direct bearing on an organization's productivity and cost. For example, we know that:

- At least one month of productivity is lost per year per employee if that person is not properly trained or supported on information systems.

- Two thirds of help desk calls would have been resolved through training.

- The cost of *not* training and supporting IT users is six times greater than training and supporting.

The role of the Computer Support professional is more important than ever. The field is growing at unprecedented rates. The hundreds of thousands of people in this field are making a significant bottom line difference. They are also dealing with the most valuable and important company resource of all—the customer.

Stop now and view the following video presentation on the Interactive Learning CD-ROM (Supplemental):

Customer Satisfaction

Overview

Customer-Centered Service

THE CUSTOMER

The value of a customer is the most precious asset that a business possesses. The customer should be at the center of all activities and be the reason that processes and products exist. An organization is literally defined by the "moments of truth" in dealing with customers. However, as organizations get larger and products and services more diverse, the once vital link to the customer can get clouded, too bureaucratic, or even lost. Customers can become problems to deal with as opposed to the essence of the business.

As computer support professionals, you deal with customers every day. Your goal is to provide the highest-quality service to these people who have made a commitment to your company. This is not only the proper professional stance, it has very real economic impact and return on investment (ROI). There is now a considerable amount of evidence to underscore just how important customers are to organizations. A summary of these findings are included below (Zemke, 1995).

It takes five times more investment to get a new customer than to retain an old one. This can vary from two to 30 times depending on complexity and size of sale.

Customers whose complaints were quickly and efficiently satisfied are actually more likely to purchase additional products than those who experienced no problems. For example, research at National Car Rental found the probability of renewal for a satisfied customer to be 85%, while a customer with a problem quickly resolved will have a 90% probability of renewal.

The *lifetime value of a customer* is a very valuable statistic. By keeping customers satisfied, they stay with the organization. If a customer is lost, this drain is significant in both reputation and dollars.

- In the automotive industry, the lifetime value of a satisfied "Ford customer" is approximately $150,000.

- As a business traveler, the *yearly* value of a customer to a hotel chain is approximately $6,500.

- A customer who has been with you for five years can be up to 377% more profitable than a new customer.

- By reducing customer defections by 5%, pre-tax profits can increase from 25 to 125%.

TOP TEN SERVICE EXPECTATIONS

Even with a strong commitment to the customer, the computer support professional has plenty to do. Whether supporting your own or third-party products to internal or external customers, problems arise. These are complex products that are distributed to a diverse audience. We know that, on average, 30% of customers service problems are not problems at all, but "user interpretation or error." While it would be pleasant to conjure an error free situation, this is not nor will it be the reality. Our job, then is to solve present and future problems as efficiently and effectively as possible.

Customers don't expect a perfect world either. Once a problem has occurred, customers have a strong set of expectations on what should occur next. These expectations go beyond (just) fixing the problem, but relate directly to *how* the problem is fixed and *how* they are treated during the process. Linda Cooper (Cooper and Associates) has researched customer service expectations and has determined that seven of the top ten service expectations relate to the recovery process. These ten expectations are targeted to the banking industry, but are relevant to most industry segments.

1. Being called back when promised
2. Receiving an explanation on how a problem happened
3. Knowing who to contact with a problem
4. Being contacted promptly when a problem is resolved
5. Being allowed to talk to someone in authority
6. Being told how long it will take to resolve a problem
7. Being given useful alternatives if a problem can't be solved

8. Being treated like a person, not an account number

9. Being told about ways to prevent a future problem

10. Being given progress reports if a problem can't be solved immediately

These basic findings are reconfirmed in a variety of other research and evaluation studies. Zemke (1995) conducted focus groups and telephone surveys with over 1,200 customers to determine the most memorable aspects of service recovery once a problem has occurred. The importance of interpersonal skills are clearly evident in this data.

Customer Service Rep (CSR)	% of Interviewees impressed by this Action
1. Dealt with my upset	79%
2. Apologized	69.1%
3. Didn't become defensive but showed humility and poise	62.9%
4. Followed up after the complaint transaction	56.8%
5. Showed skill at problem solving	53%
6. Acted in a fully responsible and empowered fashion on the customer's behalf	40.7%
7. Showed good interpersonal skills, particularly listening	40.7%

Source: *Service Recovery*

Ron Zemke, Productivity Press, 1995

CUSTOMER INTERACTION SKILLS

This treatment of Customer Interaction Skills is based firmly on the customer. Several models will be presented, and in each one, the customer is at the center. The reasons are clear. We all work for the customer; and the economics of customer service and customer retention are indisputable. In addition, it seems apparent that with responsive, quality service not only can problems be overcome, but customers will have a higher degree of loyalty to people and organizations who help them solve these problems.

The data and our own experience point to three sets of core competencies that are keys to successful computer support and service. These skills are:

- technical
- troubleshooting
- communication

The technical skills are hard to attain, ever-changing, and probably the easiest to classify. They require a knowledge of hardware, software, networks, and applications as a foundation. The technical skills provide the substance or the "what" of computer support and service. The "how" is often a combination of troubleshooting and communication skills.

Troubleshooting is the systematic process used to analyze and resolve a problem. No matter how much knowledge you possess, you won't be able to meet customer needs and expectations without troubleshooting skills. These are important tools of the trade.

Communication skills are part of the competency set because people are involved throughout the process. Even if you solve the problem yet convey the message poorly, you have not been successful. The three skill sets are all necessary, but each by itself is insufficient to achieve the end result. The competencies must all work together.

The Three Core Competencies

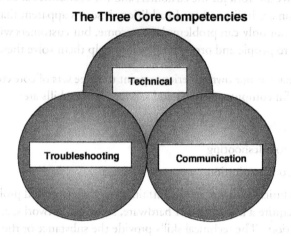

SUMMARY

In this chapter, we examined the increasing need for high-quality computer support in the workplace. We also detailed the important connection between customer expectations for service and customer retention. Finally, we noted the necessity of mastering all three core skill sets—technical, troubleshooting, and communication—to providing the desired level of service.

In the next chapters, the Wave DIReCtional Troubleshooting Model is presented. This will be an important guide for computer support professionals. Then a series of vital communication skills are discussed and linked to the troubleshooting model.

A set of case scenario exercises enable you to apply your technical, troubleshooting and communication skills to real-world situations. This treatment of Customer Interaction Skills—together with the technical courses in this curriculum—will hopefully enable you to be better prepared for the complete requirements of being an outstanding computer support and service professional.

POST-TEST QUESTIONS

The answers to these questions are in Appendix A at the end of this manual.

1. What two processes can prevent system downtime?

   ....

   ....

2. The most valuable corporate asset is _____.

   ....

   ....

3. Customers want their problem solved quickly, but even more important is _____ the problem is resolved.

   ....

   ....

4. List three common service expectations.

   ....

   ....

5. Which skill set is as important as technical knowledge?

   ....

   ....

The Customer Service Organization

▶ MAJOR TOPICS

Objectives 16

Pre-Test Questions 16

Introduction 17

Organizational Structure 18

Help Desk Challenges 20

Summary 23

Post-Test Questions 23

OBJECTIVES

At the completion of this chapter, you will be able to:

- Compare and contrast the most typical customer service organizations, along with their strengths and limitations.

- Create the essential elements and policies for an effective support environment.

PRE-TEST QUESTIONS

The answers to these questions are in Appendix A at the end of this manual.

1. Identify the most common organizational infrastructures for customer service.

   ....

   ....

2. What types of challenges do customer service professionals face daily?

   ....

   ....

3. Why are customer database records such a valuable asset?

   ....

   ....

INTRODUCTION

The customer service organization provides the framework within which the skill sets discussed in the last chapter are applied. The various types of customer service organizations lend themselves to particular customer environments, but all have the same foundation: providing the best possible support to the customer. Whether over the phone, in person, or at a service center, the support professional must be able to meet this challenge.

Certain fundamental principles of organization are useful whatever the structure. Implementing these principles can help a support environment run more smoothly and efficiently, saving you from future headaches in the process. Some of these principles are merely the establishment of good personal habits of organization, such as keeping important information visible and within reach; others require a more departmental- or area-based approach for use, such as designing appropriate and efficient database queries and escalation policies. In all cases, these principles of organization enable you to plan ahead and to make general decisions about how support will be provided in advance, instead of when frustrated customers are waiting for help.

Stop now and view the following video presentation on the Interactive Learning CD-ROM (Supplemental):

Customer Satifaction

Communication Skills

ORGANIZATIONAL STRUCTURE

Every organization designs its customer service infrastructure to best service the needs of its audience. However, three primary classifications are used most often to define most customer service organizations:

- Telephone Help Desk
- Field Service Support
- Depot Service

These three customer service types can be combined to provide the best service mix for your customers.

Telephone Help Desk

The telephone help desk is organized to provide an immediate response to your customers' requests and problems from around the corner or around the world. The significant advantage of the telephone help desk is that it can provide coverage over a broad geographic range. Customers can easily access a 1-800 number or a 1-900 number for charged activities; and a growing percentage of help desk activities use the Internet, not the telephone.

From the customer's perspective, the most frequent issue with telephone help desk support is responsiveness. It is imperative that a customer talk or interact with a help desk professional immediately. If a customer is routed to voice mail and hours of "telephone tag" ensue, then there is a high likelihood of distress. Most successful telephone help desk groups set a standard for responsiveness of no more than 1 to 2 hours.

From the help desk professional's perspective, the physical isolation from the customer and the source of the problem can present unique challenges. Both troubleshooting and interpersonal rapport must be established over the phone. While a variety of hardware, software technology, and other job aids can assist in these tasks, the fact remains that customer service must be provided without a true picture of the person or the problem.

Help Desks can be organized in numerous ways: by customer, industry group, geography, or level of technical expertise of the computer support professional. Because of its economic and geographic advantages for businesses, there are more help desk professionals than field service or depot service professionals in the marketplace.

Field Service Organization

Field service is face-to-face support. As the name implies, this support is usually provided by a dedicated organization traveling to customer sites. For internal support, this trip could be from one department to another. For support to external customers, the customer support will generally be provided at the customer's location.

Because external field source organizations include a number of highly skilled people, they are generally devoted to more expensive products and services. After an initial period of service to customers, field service organizations frequently charge for their services and become profit centers within their organization.

From a customer's perspective, personal service from a knowledgeable, dedicated computer support professional is the ultimate. This level is analogous to the family doctor making a house call. For the computer support professional, the key is not only technical and troubleshooting competencies, but also personal communications skills. Frequently, field service technicians are more senior than help desk or depot service professionals since they interact directly with customers at their locations. If the problem is solved, the customer is doubtlessly retained. If the problem remains, it can be a difficult situation both for the technician on the firing line and the company.

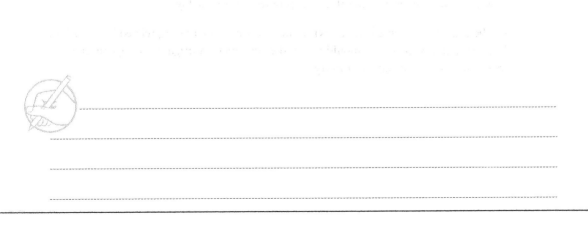

Depot Service

While depot service provides face-to-face customer service, it provides it in a different environment and context than the field service organization: customers come to the depot for support as opposed to technicians going to customers. The depot approach is usually used by retail stores or manufacturers' agents. A large number of people can be served over the course of the day by a single technician. Systems are frequently left at the depot for service or replacement, and retrieved several days later.

It is not uncommon for organizations to use at least two of these approaches to providing customer service. Each approach has its own strengths and role in the marketplace. Each uses the same foundation, but also slightly different troubleshooting and communications skills described in subsequent chapters.

HELP DESK CHALLENGES

Successful help desks are organized to combine established processes with flexible adjustment ranges to provide customers the highest quality service. Many of these topics are also treated in the chapter on the DIReCtional troubleshooting process, but they are also summarized here. The following five points are organizational suggestions to help build effective customer service rapport.

Balance Paperwork and Customer Urgency

A documented audit trail is one of the most important troubleshooting tools. Many customers are so frantic that they do not realize that what seems like administrative activity will help you understand their problem better and will allow you fix the problem more quickly. An effective response to an uncooperative customer could be, "Sir/Ma'am, these questions help me understand your specific configuration. If you can help me answer them, I will be able to solve your problem more quickly."

The help desk is not an effective environment to gather marketing-related information. The introductory questions should reflect the customer's configuration, operational system activities, and account history.

Establish a Structured Escalation Policy

It is essential that documented procedures outline the appropriate actions to be taken in the case of a major service outage. Questions that need to be addressed include:

- How does your customer define a major service outage (number of workstations, designated server outage, access to a mission critical application)?
- What resources are available to assist with the problem resolution?
- What determines the need to escalate (designated time intervals, specific error messages)?
- Who is the primary point of contact for both vendor and customer?
- Is there a contingency plan in place to contact all people who are required to authorize system recovery decisions?
- How does the changeover to backup or parallel systems occur?
- Is a trouble log maintained?
- Is a centralized list of support phone numbers and customer identification information compiled?

Review all Customer-Related Documentation

An automated customer database can assist you in tracking trends specific to your client or related products. Be prepared. Understand the previous support activities associated with your client's organization so that you can identify a common problem, or spot a trend relating to intermittent trouble activity. Knowledge is power.

Help desk organizations need to establish a common set of abbreviations and conventions for documentation purposes. Otherwise, each person working on an account will utilize their personal shorthand and no one will be able to decipher any past activities.

The database query format should be designed to enable any of the help desk staff to review the most recent account activity, including any open trouble reports. The database form also should be designed for quick keyboard entry of customer information. Tabbing through unnecessary or repetitive fields can add valuable seconds to help desk response time averages.

Help desk support staff who work at the customer site must review all pertinent information before meeting the customer. Nothing is more infuriating than repeating a story four or five times to people within the same organization. After all, should your customer need to organize your internal communications?

Maintain an Orderly Work Area

Information is a very powerful tool, as long as you know where to go to obtain it. Maintaining an orderly work area helps you to maintain a clear perspective and a level head during moments of crisis. Being able to immediately access the required information will speed the problem resolution process dramatically.

Some information to keep within easy reach is:

- The top ten common problems and associated resolutions.
- Escalation procedures and contact phone numbers.
- Vendor contact information.
- Unresolved intermittent problems and possible fixes.

Respect all Copyright Limitations

Violating copyright restrictions is equivalent to stealing. Installing a software product that does not have the appropriate license information is both unethical and illegal. This includes temporary software installations such as virus scanners or inventory packages.

SUMMARY

Although help desks may be structured to best service their unique customer base, the overall goal of performing the highest quality customer service is central to every help desk organization. The tasks required to provide this level of quality include:

- A balance between administrative paperwork and customer urgency.
- An established escalation policy.
- Constant attention to customer records and trends.
- Well managed work areas.
- Enforcement of copyright requirements.

POST-TEST QUESTIONS

The answers to these questions are in Appendix A at the end of this manual.

1. Briefly describe the different characteristics of telephone help desks, field service support, and depot service.

   ....

   ....

2. List four escalation plan parameters.

   ....

   ....

3. Before beginning diagnostic activities, what task must be completed?

   ....

   ....

4. What two resource items would you keep within easy reach to best support your customers?

....

....

5. Are computer support professionals excused from observing copyright protections?

....

....

CHAPTER ③

DIReCtional Troubleshooting

MAJOR TOPICS

Objectives 26

Pre-Test Questions... 26

Introduction 27

Define the Problem.. 29

Isolate the Problem 36

Resolve the Problem 38

Confirm the Resolution and Expectations.................... 42

Broadcast the Solution....................................... 44

Document the Final Findings 44

Summary 45

Post-Test Questions 46

OBJECTIVES

At the completion of this chapter, you will be able to:

- Identify the components of the troubleshooting cycle.
- Gather information relevant to a support problem according to the six questions: who, what , when, where, why, and how.
- Determine the specific system information relevant to a problem.
- Reproduce and isolate the problem under controlled conditions.
- Apply research of both internal and external sources to the resolution of the problem.
- Communicate the essential details of the solution to the customer and the full details to other support personnel.
- Help your troubleshooting efforts and assure customer rapport by consistently involving the customer at the appropriate times.
- Maintain necessary documentation during each step of the problem-solving process.

PRE-TEST QUESTIONS

The answers to these questions are in Appendix A at the end of this manual.

1. What are the four basic phases of the troubleshooting cycle?

   ....

   ....

2. What resources are effective research tools?

   ....

   ....

3. What activities should occur when the problem is resolved?

   ....

   ....

INTRODUCTION

This proven method leads you through the complete troubleshooting procedure. Through this process you will define, isolate, and resolve the problem. You will also confirm and document your findings so that you will build your own troubleshooting reference library. As a computer support professional, these steps will be used everyday as you perform your job. Notice that the customer is in the center of the DIReCtional Model.

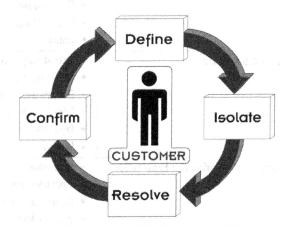

This section provides the complete step-by-step guide to troubleshooting, using Wave's DIReCtional Troubleshooting Model. This process will take you, systematically, from defining the problem to resolving it. The table below illustrates the procedures you will use in each step in the problem-solving process.

Step	In this step you will
1. Define the Problem	• Describe the problem. • Determine the problem type. • Specify the conditions. • Try a quick fix. • Document everything pertaining to the problem. • Set expectations.
2. Isolate the Occurrence	• Reproduce the problem. • Classify the problem. • Reconfirm the problem. • Document.
3. Resolve the Problem	• Research the problem. • Identify potential causes. • Eliminate unlikely causes. • Solve the problem. • Repeat the solution. • Document the resolution.
4. Confirm the Resolution and Expectations	• Review case history. • Confirm with your customer. • Communicate the solution. • Document final findings.

Stop now and view the following video presentation on the Interactive Learning CD-ROM (Supplemental):

Customer Satisfaction

Troubleshooting

DEFINE THE PROBLEM

Describe Your Customer's Problem

You will be taking notes much like a journalist does when he is in pursuit of a story. You will answer the questions: who, what, when, where, why, and how. In other words, get as much detail as you possibly can when in the defining process and it will make the other steps a little easier. When a customer approaches you with a problem, some of the questions you will ask are:

- Who

  Who is the person with the support problem? What is his or her role in the company? Is it an administrative assistant who uses the computer 6 out of 8 hours in the day? Is it an occasional user who only uses his or her computer a few times a week?

- What

  What specifically is the problem and what equipment is involved? Try to narrow this down to a simple paragraph statement. For example, a problem statement might indicate that "the laser printer in the accounting department will not print form letters from Microsoft Word generated from user A's computer."

- When

  When did the problem occur? Is this the first time the problem occurred? Does this happen all the time? Is the problem intermittent (only happen sometimes)? Does it resolve itself when the computer is rebooted? Does it occur if there are many users on the network? Try to get your customer to be very specific about when the problem occurs.

- Where

  Where is the problem? What department of the company? Where is the equipment located? What floor of the building? Where is the user located?

- Why

  Why is the problem occurring? Sometimes the user may have an indication as to why he is experiencing problems. You might ask your customer something like, "Do you think you might know why you are experiencing problems?"

- How

  How is the problem occurring? Can you duplicate it? Can your customer tell you in detail how the problem happened and what she did just prior to that?

Use the following table as a handy summary checklist:

✓ Problem Description

Ask your customer	To determine
❑ **Who**	• Who is the customer (and what is her title and role in the organization)?
❑ **What**	• What is the exact problem? • What is the result? • What is on the screen? • What was your customer doing when the problem occurred?
❑ **When**	• When did the problem occur?
❑ **Where**	• Where is the problem? (What department of the company?) • Where is the equipment located? (What floor of the building?) • Where is the user located?
❑ **Why**	• Why is the problem occurring?
❑ **How**	• How is the problem occurring?

Determine the Problem Type

If you can solve the customer's problem on the first call, you will have a satisfied customer. The easiest solution is one that you have already resolved. The first check, then, is to determine the problem type.

Is this a known problem?

Review existing documentation files. Your troubleshooting reference library is a collection of technical manuals, inventory records, trouble logs, as well as frequently asked questions, and their resolutions (FAQ). If a similar problem occurred previously, you may be able to use the same solution and solve the customer's problem immediately. It is important to document every incident so you can expand the contents of your troubleshooting reference library and maintain the currency of your information. Constant documentation also allows you to recognize trends and diagnose a system-wide problem that may initially appear to be a series of unrelated incidents.

Is this an unknown problem?

Try to locate the problem in your troubleshooting reference library. If the problem has not occurred before and is not documented, document it now and give as much detail as possible.

Specify All Conditions

You will want to check all conditions that apply to your customer's hardware, software, and environment. It is imperative to be as specific as possible because in order to solve a problem, it must be duplicated. These conditions are instrumental to the process of duplicating the problem.

Check this	To verify
❑ **Hardware**	Exactly what equipment was your customer using? (Was she running an application on her computer with a networked or stand-alone printer?) Make certain to list all of the hardware involved. Here are some things to list: • Processor (manufacturer, model number, clock speed) • Addressable RAM memory • Usable hard-disk space, Video specifications (manufacturer, family, resolution) • Monitor specifications (manufacturer, size, resolution) • Add-ins. This includes additional drives, modems, application cards, etc. • Network interfaces (manufacturer, network type and version, configuration)
❑ **Software**	What programs are installed on your customer's system? Were they in a Windows application? Did she have several programs open on her desktop? Did she toggle from a Windows application to a DOS application? Make certain to list all applications installed on your customer's computer such as: • Operating system (such as Windows NT) • Networking system (such as Novell v4.1) • User applications (MS Word, MS Office, WordPerfect, etc.) • Open applications
❑ **Environment**	Always indicate what physical environment the equipment was in. Was it in a clean, virtually dust-free surrounding (perhaps a laboratory), or in a cluttered office area? Checking the equipment's environment will go a long way in trying to diagnose the problem. List all conditions: • Connections • Clean/Dusty • Hot/Cold environment • Power source • Time of day

A Quick Fix

Even if the problem is unknown, there may be some immediate fixes that will solve the problem or at least some aspect of the problem. For example, if your customer tells you that the networked printer has not worked at all today you might tell your customer to first check the cables and connections. Then, if that doesn't work, you might want to instruct your customer to reset the printer. Remember, a "quick fix" may be all that is required. Based on our experience, here are some quick fixes that have often worked.

✓ Quick Fix Hit List

❑ Check the connectors
❑ Check all power switches
❑ Check system resources
❑ Check available memory
❑ New hardware installed lately
❑ System software installed lately
❑ Reset workstation

Document Everything

Write down as much of the problem as you possibly can. This will help you build your own troubleshooting reference library, and will help you resolve any future occurrences.

Leaving a documentation audit trail is one of the most important things you can do to ensure that your customer gets the service they deserve. Document what is on the screen, as well as characteristics of system performance.

✓ Documentation Audit Trail Checklist

❑ **Screen error code**
❑ **Concurrent applications**
❑ **Frequency of the error**
❑ **Percentage of system affected**
❑ **Preliminary triage steps**
❑ **Next activity**

Set Expectations

When does your customer need a resolution? Is the company in the middle of a critical project with an immediate deadline? Work with your customer to establish what must be accomplished to resolve the immediate situation and what can be handled as secondary concerns. If you need to juggle several time-critical customer problems, never let on that one customer is any less of a priority than another.

Always relay the customer's expectation back to him so there are no surprises.

✓ Documenting Customer Expectations

❑ **Nature of the problem**
❑ **Challenge to overcome**
❑ **Time frame requirements**
❑ **Interim solution**
❑ **Customer concurrence**

ISOLATE THE PROBLEM

The importance of this step is that it is essential to be able to reproduce the problem before it can be solved. The logical troubleshooting process can proceed once the problem has been isolated.

✓ Problem Isolation Checklist

❑ **Can the problem be recreated?**
❑ **Is this a common occurance?**
❑ **Is the problem intermittent?**
❑ **Did you reconfirm interim findings with your customer?**

Reproduce the Problem

The first step is to repeat the conditions (as reported by your customer) to see if the problem reoccurs. You must repeat the conditions exactly.

The process of duplicating the situation as a part of the isolation problem solving phase allows you to begin a methodical approach using deductive reasoning techniques.

Classify the Problem

After you duplicate your customer's conditions, you will list, or "classify" the problem by how frequently it occurs, and if it can be consistently duplicated.

Intermittent

An intermittent problem is one that happens infrequently, and without any logical time sequence. In other words, it may occur once, then not again for another day, then it may happen intermittently five times in one day. These are the toughest types of problems to solve; and they require cycling back to define the problem more completely.

Duplicateable

A duplicateable problem is one that happens at logical intervals and consistently when the user performs the same action. It could also happen at logical and consistent time sequences. For example, if a customer tries to print a very large document and the printer produces garbled text from just that one document, that problem is "duplicateable."

Reconfirm the Problem with the Customer

After determining the problem, you will present the identified malfunction to the customer for her review. The customer also needs to be made aware of problems that appear to be intermittent and have no long-term resolution.

Document the Status

Is this problem totally resolved, or do you have more research to do? At this stage, the simple problems and the known problems have probably been resolved. The more complex problems will require research and more in-depth activity. If the problem is intermittent, you will certainly have to communicate with the customer, probably after doing research that is discussed in the next step.

RESOLVE THE PROBLEM

It may be that in duplicating the customer's condition, you may have already resolved the problem and documented the status as complete. However, you may find that you have to refer to outside sources and additional reference material, and this may become a more detailed search for a resolution.

Research the Problem

You may have to refer to more than one resource when you research the problem. There are two types of resources you will use: Internal and External. Here are descriptions of both types of resources.

Internal Resources

Internal resources pertain to anything within your organization that you can use as a reference guide. This includes, but is not limited to:

- On-site files and records

  You will refer to past records and files of the same or similar situations. This is why it is *vital* to document every occurrence properly, and to build your own troubleshooting reference library.

- Contacts with suppliers

  The relationships you build with your suppliers are extremely important. These people are a wealth of knowledge when it comes to the products they represent. Use your contact with suppliers as solid reference materials.

- Reference materials

  Original and supplemental manufacturer's manuals can be a tremendous help to you in troubleshooting. These manuals and reference materials supply important information for data such as dip switch settings, etc. Many times a help desk phone number is listed inside the reference. Never discard any reference material, as it can be a valuable tool in resolving future problems.

External Resources

- Network with like professionals

  Never underestimate the power of networking with professionals in your field. These people are a rich pocket of information and freely share their knowledge and expertise with others in a similar profession. Many regions throughout the country have organizations geared toward those in your profession–consider joining a professional group. If there is no group in your area, you might want to start one.

- The Internet

  The Internet is a tool that millions of people use on a daily basis to get information from product literature to baseball scores. Many people have found the Internet to be so useful as an information tool, that it is one of the first resources they will use. Many of the larger companies (like Microsoft) have very helpful information in their FAQ (frequently asked questions) section. This section is packed full of all sorts of helpful advice on a vast array of products. Based on our experience, here are some very useful sites.

Internet Technical Resources

www.microsoft.com	Microsoft Corporation
www.intel.com	Intel Corporation
www.mot.com	Motorola Corporation
www.sun.com	Sun Microsystems
www.ibm.com	IBM Corporation
www.apple.com	Apple Corporation
www.digital.com	Digital Equipment Corporation
www.seagate.com	Seagate Technology
www.compaq.com	Compaq Computer Corporation
www.hp.com	Hewlett-Packard Corporation
www.usr.com	US Robotics
www.zdnet.com	Ziff-Davis Publishing
www.packardbell.com	Packard-Bell Corporation
www.wavetech.com	Wave Technologies
www.comptia.org	CompTIA
www.microsoft.com/support	Microsoft Support
ftp.microsoft.com/services/ msedcert/e&cmap.zip	Microsoft Roadmap
http://support.novell.com/	Novell Support
http://www.novell.com/nui	Novell Users Forum on the Web

In addition to these technical resources on the Internet, you will want to use search engines to access other sources. Two of the most useful are the following:

LookSmart   at   www.looksmart.com

MetaCrawler   at   www.metacrawler.com

Identify Potential Causes and Eliminate the Improbable

Take a methodical approach to identify potential causes to a problem. Make a list of potential causes. After you make your list of potential causes, start eliminating them one-by-one. Start with the most obvious, least intrusive causes and then work your way down your list. By starting with the more likely causes, you stand a better chance of a quick resolution.

Solve the Problem

Once you have eliminated the improbable causes, you are ready to begin a systematic search for the solution. By systematically testing, then eliminating those items remaining on your *potential cause* list, you will find that you will be able to duplicate the problem efficiently, without duplicating your efforts.

Repeat/QC Solution

After you solve the problem, make certain that you repeat it in order to test the system solution/fix. By repeating the process, you are verifying that the problem was what you thought it was, and validating the solution. This step is very important and often overlooked. There is a strong temptation to rush a solution to the customer. However, if the solution does not work or is only a partial fix, then the customer will become really upset. QC is vital to customer satisfaction.

Document the Resolution

Always document your resolution. By documenting the process you used to resolve the problem, you are building your own database within your troubleshooting reference library. Many times this is the most important and reliable resource you will have.

✓ Problem Resolution Checklist

❑ **Current hypothesis**
❑ **Available research sources**
❑ **Final problem resolution**
❑ **Systems assurance testing**
❑ **Customer comments**
❑ **Complete documentation of problem resolution activities**

CONFIRM THE RESOLUTION AND EXPECTATIONS

This is the last step in the DIReCtional Troubleshooting Model, and one that will give you and your customer closure to the problem. Additionally, this step will help build your customer's confidence in your ability as a professional. Never eliminate this step in the process. To confirm problem resolution, perform the following:

Review Case History

After you resolve the problem, make certain that you thoroughly review all documentation and events leading up to a solution. Is this a common, more classic case? If it is common, does the problem seem to occur in this type of hardware/software? Remember, sometimes you will be the only source in your organization that has this vital information, so perform a thorough and accurate review.

Confirm with the Customer

After you have resolved the problem and thoroughly reviewed its case history, then you can confirm your results to the customer. It is absolutely critical that you confirm your findings with your customer. This will bolster your customer's confidence in you as a support professional, and set you apart from other support personnel in your field. Communicate the following to your customer:

Repeat the problem back to the customer as the customer conveyed the original information to you. This will let the customer reconfirm the problem.

Review the solution with the customer. Briefly describe why the problem occurred, what you did to solve the problem, and perhaps how the problem could be avoided in the future. This also is the appropriate time to review productivity issues that could affect end user or system performance. Do not forget to remind customers of any relevant service bulletins from product manufacturers that include upgrade or other product maintenance information.

Open Service Calls

If the problem resolution cannot be immediately implemented because of equipment shipment delays or other circumstances, it is even more important to maintain a good rapport. Confirm your customer understands the reason why the problem is not resolved and the next step in the problem resolution process. This information could be a delivery date or the name of the third-tier service technician who will install the software patch.

BROADCAST THE SOLUTION

Communicate common problems with the rest of your group or organization. Many times, you are the only source of information on the problem and its solution and your customers depend on you to communicate that to them.

By broadcasting the solution to your customers, you also play a key role in future purchases and processes used in your organization. Personnel making buying decisions will also have to know if a particular piece of equipment seems to have consistent problems. The information you provide to them will be a tremendous help in their decisions, and may save your organization time and money.

Here are some of the vehicles that you can use to communicate solutions:

- Monthly newsletters–Include handy items such as a "tip-of-the-month" section
- Your organization's intranet or bulletin board system
- Group e-mails

DOCUMENT THE FINAL FINDINGS

Document any suggestions that you gave to your customer, his comments, and any final findings. Once you document the final findings, you may then file them in your troubleshooting reference library for future use.

SUMMARY

These, then, are the four steps in the Wave DIReCtional troubleshooting model. This model has been distilled from the literature and our own experience. We are confident that it can help you be successful as a computer support professional. As always, the customer–both internal and external–is right at the center of this process.

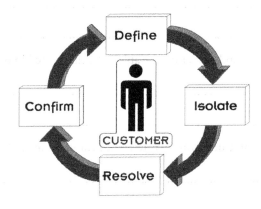

POST-TEST QUESTIONS

The answers to these questions are in Appendix A at the end of this manual.

1. What are the six questions that need to be asked when helping your customer describe a problem?

   ....

   ....

2. What conditions must be able to be duplicated in order to resolve a problem?

   ....

   ....

3. List three questions that reference common quick fix solutions.

   ....

   ....

4. What diagnostic step is common across all four DIReCtional phases?

   ....

   ....

5. List three vehicles you can use to communicate innovative solutions.

   ....

   ....

Communication Skills

Objectives 48

Pre-Test Questions.. 48

Introduction 49

Effective Listening Techniques.................................... 50

Questioning Skills.. 53

Handling Difficult Situations 56

Setting Expectations 58

Following Up 60

Compile Frequently Asked Questions 63

Summary 64

Post-Test Questions 64

CHAPTER 4

OBJECTIVES

At the completion of this chapter, you will be able to:

- Listen effectively to your customer's concerns, issues, and particulars.
- Use both close- and open-ended questions so as to gather and confirm information effectively.
- Apply the five-step ALERT process when faced with a frustrated or angry customer.
- Set reasonable expectations for yourself and the resources available to you, and communicate these to your customer.
- Perform necessary follow-up activities for your benefit, your customer's, and the support organization's.

PRE-TEST QUESTIONS

The answers to these questions are in Appendix A at the end of this manual.

1. Identify the five professional communication skill sets that are essential for success as a computer support professional.

    ....

    ....

2. List three face-to-face skill sets that help establish a positive rapport.

    ....

    ....

3. What is the #1 rule to remember when handling an angry or frustrated customer?

    ....

    ....

INTRODUCTION

One of the key ingredients to becoming an expert troubleshooter is knowing how to communicate with your customer so that you can understand and respond to his concerns. The three important skill sets for a world-class computer support professional are technical knowledge, troubleshooting, and communications skills. All three are prerequisites for success.

In this section you will learn how to effectively interact with your customer by using key interpersonal skills. The following diagram shows these vital communication skills.

EFFECTIVE LISTENING TECHNIQUES

To effectively serve your customer, you must *actively* practice effective listening skills. This is not as easy as it seems. Listening is hard work. However, to be effective in your job, it is absolutely mandatory. First, it shows the customer that you care. Second, you must listen to gain the information you need to solve the problem. Third, it can help build a trust relationship with the customer that has direct business impact.

A useful listening guideline is "to put yourself in the customer's shoes." Try to understand his situation, as well as his problems. Even go to the extent of trying to visualize them, if you are communicating by phone. Customers deserve your full attention.

A barrier to effective listening is that you think you already know the answer and cut the customer off in mid-sentence. In other situations, you shut down listening and start rehearsing your answer while the customer is still talking. This is unfair to you and the customer. Recognize his expertise with regard to the situation. You may miss important information and the customer deserves to be heard, uninterrupted.

Evaluate the knowledge level of your customer and respond to his comments and queries respectfully. Do not "talk down" or use patronizing terms. Explain the problem and resolution using clear and easily understood language.

On the following pages are some guidelines for face-to-face and telephone communications.

Face-to-Face Techniques

Your customer needs to know that you genuinely care about his support issue and that you are going to take positive steps to resolve his problem. Here are the key elements in practicing effective face-to-face techniques.

Greet Customer

When you arrive at your customer's location, greet your customer(s) with a smile, a confident attitude, and a firm handshake. Initial positive customer contact is essential for both internal and external clients.

First appearances are very important. Dress in a clean, neat, and professional manner at all times.

Maintain Eye Contact

Eye contact shows your customer that you are focused on him and his concerns. This does not mean that you have to stare at him. However, when talking to your customer, do not let your eyes "wander" at other things in the room, such as looking at objects outside a window.

Always maintain steady eye contact with your customer throughout the entire conversation.

Exercise Positive Body Language

Here are a few of the ways you can show your customer that you are paying attention to him:

- Demonstrate good posture. As simple as this sounds, it is important.
- Be attentive, avoid distractions such as listening to other nearby conversations.

Display visual reinforcements. One of the ways your customer knows that you acknowledge his problem is by visual confirmation. So, while your customer explains his problem, nod your head and adjust your facial expression every few moments to let him know you are "hearing" him.

Practice Thorough Note Taking

Never commit an issue to memory. Always make a habit to write down as much of your customer's concerns or issues as you possibly can. This will not only show your customer that you care, but it will be a tremendous help to you if you have several projects going at one time.

Telephone Techniques

Since your customer cannot see your facial expressions while trying to explain her problem over the telephone, the techniques you use in your telephone conversations will be quite different from those you use in face-to-face communication.

Here are the key points to follow when you engage in a telephone conversation with your customer.

Practice Active Listening

Your customer needs to know that you are actively listening to her problem. Ask for clarification often, and do not hesitate to summarize what you hear back to the customer, for clarification.

Remain Calm and Use Rules of Telephone Etiquette

There will be instances when your customer becomes extremely frustrated, and passes the point of sound reason. You can play a key part in calming your customer by talking in a very pleasant manner. When you use a pleasant tone, you are relaying to your customer not to panic.

Remember, your customer relies upon you to solve the problem and to be a voice of authority.

Exercise Verbal Confirmation

Your customer needs to know that you understand exactly what she is trying to relay to you about her problem. So you must give your customer a verbal confirmation in the conversation, and then repeat the problem at the end of the conversation.

For example, during the conversation you interject with, "I understand," or "yes." Then, at the end of the conversation, recap what the customer just told you in a brief form. Your conversation might go something like, "So, to review what you just said, you cannot reset your computer using the control, alt and delete keys after several attempts, is that correct?" Then, let the customer confirm that this is the problem.

QUESTIONING SKILLS

The second key communication skill that is used in conjunction with the DIReCtional troubleshooting model is questioning. Effective questioning techniques, coupled with good listening habits, will enable you to resolve problems more quickly by focusing and redirecting conversations with your customer.

The two main types of questioning techniques are open- and close-ended questions. These questions can be used independently or in conjunction with each other.

Open-Ended Questioning Techniques

An open-ended question is one that, when asked, gives your customer the unlimited freedom to answer as she wishes. An open-ended question cannot be answered with a yes or no. Answers to these questions may be very short or very long, depending on how customers choose to answer the question.

An example of an open-ended question is, "Why do you think the problem occurred?" The answer to this question might be as simple as "I don't know," or it might be a very long and detailed response.

Using Open-Ended Questions for Information Gathering

During the initial phase of the conversation, try to get as much of your customer's feedback by asking open-ended questions. This technique will help you in your quest to gather as much information about the problem as possible. It also enables the customer to contribute, lets her know you are interested in what she has to say, and provides you with vital information.

Close-Ended Questioning Techniques

A close-ended question is very different than an open-ended question. In this question you will pose your question as more of a statement, then ask for a "yes" or "no" confirmation; or you will ask a question that has a simple yes or no answer.

In this type of question, you try to limit your customer's response, and be more focused in your questioning efforts. An example of a close-ended question is, "Were the cables properly connected?"

Using Close-Ended Questions to Gather Information and Confirm

Use a close-ended question when you are giving your customer confirmation that you understand the scope of the problem. An example of a close-ended statement is, "You cannot get your printer to go on line. Is that correct?" Your customer will respond with either a "yes" or "no" answer.

It is good practice to *follow* an open-ended question with several close-ended questions based on what the customer said in the open-ended response. This practice reinforces the fact that you are interested in what the customer is saying, and it focuses your troubleshooting efforts.

Close-ended questions should also be used to reconfirm major points with the customer. This use will help set customer expectations and clarify communications. For example, you may want to use a question such as the following:

"If I call you back Tuesday at 10:00 with an answer, is that fine?"

The customer answers yes or no and expectations are firmly established.

Comparing Open- and Close-Ended Questions

The table below outlines typical close- and open-ended questions. The first three examples illustrate how a simple word change can solicit a broader response that clarifies the situation.

Sometimes close-ended questions are necessary to identify the computing environment. The second group of questions illustrates how open-ended questions can be used to expand the initial response from your customer to better understand the goals that she is trying to accomplish.

Close-Ended Question	Sample Answer	Open-Ended Question	Sample Answer
Can you describe the visual image on your monitor screen?	Yes	What does the visual image on your monitor screen resemble?	There are rows of garbled letters.
Can you access the inventory control program?	No	What happens when you try to access the inventory control program?	I click on the icon and then immediately get an error message 52 that tells me that the data file can't be found.
Can you describe what happens when you try to dial into the headquarters network?	Yes	What happens when you try to dial into the headquarters network?	I can get through to the modem connection, but then I can't login.
Which directory did you designate for the Web page download?	C:\stuff	Why did you designate that particular directory to receive the Internet files?	Because, I wanted to keep my data files separate from the browser program......
What settings did you set for the jumpers?	2 and 4	Why did you choose non-standard settings for the jumpers?	Because, I have a sound card and I didn't want to give them both the same settings.....
Which port are you using for your modem?	Com1	Why did you choose Com1 for your modem port?	I don't know......

HANDLING DIFFICULT SITUATIONS

In the course of your job, there will be difficult situations that arise. Not all problems can be easily resolved. Your customers depend on information technology and when it does not work, they can get frustrated and angry. This condition is part of the job, just as the thanks and appreciation for solving a problem is part of the job.

No matter how competent you are or how hard you work, you will not be able to solve every problem or satisfy every customer. This 100% level must be your goal but you will not be able to consistently achieve it. The key is to recognize this fact, stay professional, and not get frustrated.

Be ALERT!

The following set of steps have proved to be very useful in dealing with difficult situations.

- **A**cknowledge
- **L**isten
- **E**mpathize
- **R**espond
- **T**hank

Here's an acronym to help you remember the key aspects of customer relations.

Acknowledge

Nobody likes to wait, not knowing when they will be helped. Always promptly return messages acknowledging that you know there is a problem, that the customer is important, and that you will take care of him or her. Prioritizing your time and emergencies is very important. Many customers will understand that you can't drop everything to take care of them immediately, but they do want a general idea of when they can expect you.

If a customer leaves you a voice or electronic mail message, acknowledge that you received it. If you are working on solving a customer problem, let her know how you are progressing.

Listen

Always actively listen to the customer with the goal of understanding. Many times when the customer begins describing a problem, our minds will rush ahead trying to determine the most appropriate response. Always wait, and listen to the whole conversation.

Empathize

After you have listened to the customer, it's equally important to empathize with the customer. Put yourself in his/her shoes. Why is he upset? What are his concerns? How does this effect his job? How would you feel if this happened to you? We've all had situations where we were uncomfortable, frustrated, unproductive. How did you feel? How did you want to be treated? Sometimes we all just need someone to say, "I understand that this is a frustrating experience."

Respond

After listening and empathizing, it is important that we respond to the customer. Responding isn't always immediately firing off a solution. You may choose to begin by asking open-ended questions, prompting the client for more information.

This is the step where you begin to take action. After accessing all the information, let the customer know what you intend to do. Keep the customer posted during the repair process. After resolving the problem, let the customer know what you've done.

Thank

Sometimes we forget to thank the customer. "Why should I thank the customer? He should thank me for solving his problem!" Remember, you should thank the customer for giving you business. It doesn't have to be a canned response. How you issue thanks may vary with each situation. The key is to show the customer appreciation. "I appreciate your patience during this process." "Thanks for giving us a call." "Let me know if you have any other problems. I always appreciate getting out and working with our customers."

SETTING EXPECTATIONS

Quality service is defined as meeting or exceeding customer expectations. Therefore, it is vital to first define expectations for each customer. It is also important to define what you expect from the customer.

Setting reasonable expectations involves the following steps:

- Establish a working partnership with your customer.

- Promise only what you can deliver.

- Set realistic resolution time frames.

- Document commitments and dates.

- Never offer an unrealistic solution to your customer.

Although you may feel pressured into a speedy commitment, the consequences may be more than you bargained for. Always stop to consider the end goal; solving the problem and having a satisfied customer. Customers want high quality and lasting solutions, even if it takes longer to achieve than anticipated.

When there are delays to the identified time frame, contact your client and explain the situation. Continue the working partnership that you established to prioritize the activities that require an immediate alternative, and those that can wait until the situation is resolved. Don't forget to document any changes to the original schedule or configuration.

Establish a Working Partnership with Your Customer

Partner with your customer. Let your customer know that both of you are part of the solution. There may be a list of things that your customer can do to prevent the problem from occurring again. If this is so, let your customer know preventive steps that she can do for herself.

Promise Only What You Can Deliver

Do not promise the customer more than you can deliver. In other words, do not make rash promises to which you cannot possibly commit. For example, if it is outside your control, it would be unwise to promise a customer an upgrade to her Windows program or to say that you will be able to resolve the problem when you have not yet been able to duplicate it.

Set a Realistic Resolution Time Frame

When you commit to a resolution timeline, you have to consider whether you have complete control over the process.

Is this a known problem where you have a ready reference and can deliver a swift solution, or is this an unknown problem that will require a great deal of research? If the later is more likely, then you may have to use your best judgment in predicting how quickly others can respond to you.

Make certain to build in a "buffer" of time, so that you will not disappoint your customer. Always tell your customer that you may have to consult with other parties or outside sources in order to resolve the problem.

Document Commitments and Dates

Always document resolution times that you promised your customers. Do this on the original work order form, or the form that you used when the problem originated.

FOLLOWING UP

Since customer service is a continuous process, you must
always communicate with your customer to make certain
that the commitments you promised and the service you
delivered were exactly as the customer expected. This is
the follow-up process.

The follow-up process involves these steps:

- Deliver on commitments, time frames, and
  solutions.

- Ensure your customer's complete and total satisfaction.

- Solicit suggestions for service and process improvements.

- Avoid future problems by documenting problem resolution.

- Update customer records for future service and support needs.

Deliver on Commitments, Time Frames, and Solutions

Did you tell your customer that you would resolve her problem by a certain deadline? If you did, then you must make every effort to deliver in a timely manner.

Chances are that if you gave a solid date of resolution to your customer, she has already planned her commitments (projects, etc.) accordingly. For example, if you told your customer that you would resolve her problem by Tuesday, they probably planned her project deadline around that date.

So, your commitments are much like a domino effect on your customer, and they have a great impact on their productivity.

A suggestion for field service support visiting end users at their desk top location is to leave a calling card. The diagram below illustrates a sample calling card the same size as a standard business card. The information identifies the help desk specialist contact information on one side and problem resolution on the other side.

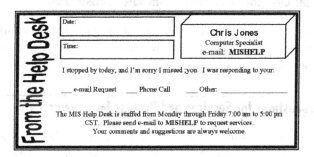

Front Side of Card

```
Your Service Call Number is _____.  The status on your call is
as follows:

____ I was able to SUCCESSFULLY complete your request to:
      _____

____ I was NOT able to complete your request due to the following:
      ____ Missing parts/supplies
      ____ Access privileges
      ____ Need more information
      ____ My next step is _____

____ Your requeset requires your presence.  We need to reschedule.
____ Please call ext. _1005_  or email MISHELP the Help Desk to discuss the call status.
```

Back Side of Card

This card serves two purposes. The first is to offer customers a document specifying the work accomplished and the status of the problem resolution. The second is that your clients in the field have a contact record with the phone numbers, electronic mail address, and a specific name (even if the help desk specialist is not dedicated).

Ensure Your Customer's Complete and Total Satisfaction

Always check with your customer to make certain that she is satisfied with your progress. Do this during the entire process so there will not be any "surprises" when you complete your work.

Solicit Suggestions for Services and Process Improvements

Many times you will be too involved in solving problems to know how your customers are using their systems. Always ask your customers for suggestions as to how they think your service and process could be improved. By doing this, you will get a fresh perspective of your customers' needs.

Avoid Future Problems by Documenting Problem Resolutions

You can avoid many problems by looking at past problem resolution documentation. For example, if an organization has several computers of one particular brand and model, and a few seem to have a common problem, you can take a proactive approach in resolving that problem by referring to prior service documentation.

This is why keeping accurate documentation is so important. Many times you will be the only person in your organization who is aware of a potential problem, and you can solve it before it drastically lowers productivity.

Update Customer Records for Future Service and Support Needs

Always keep a record your customer's service and support needs. For example, there may be a department in his organization that works in a particularly dusty environment and needs a preventive maintenance check on equipment every quarter instead of semi-annually. By keeping accurate records, you can deliver the service he needs in a timely manner while preventing potential problems.

COMPILE FREQUENTLY ASKED QUESTIONS

Keep a record of all questions that your customers ask you. You will soon notice that many customers ask the same type of question.

In order to educate all of your customers, you might want to "publish" a newsletter or a lists of FAQs (frequently asked questions). Educating your customers in this manner can go a long way to prevent future problems.

SUMMARY

These, then, are the communication skills that, together with technical and troubleshooting skills, characterize excellence in the computer support profession. No matter how technically capable you are, if you cannot communicate your ideas and solutions effectively, you will be less successful in your job. While these communication skills may seem obvious, it takes hard work and dedication to become an expert.

POST-TEST QUESTIONS

The answers to these questions are in Appendix A at the end of this manual.

1. Why is listening the most important troubleshooting skill?

    ....

    ....

2. List three telephone techniques that promote active listening.

    ....

    ....

3. Identify the following questions as closed (C) or open (O):

    _____ What was the displayed error code?

    _____ Which directory did you assign as a default?

    _____ Why did you choose this particular setup configuration?

    _____ Can you describe what other applications were open?

4. Define the ALERT acronym.

    ....

    ....

5. List the four steps to follow when setting a customers expectations.

    ....

    ....

6. Why is customer follow up an essential troubleshooting step?

    ....

    ....

Customer Interaction Skills
Case Scenarios

MAJOR TOPICS

Objectives...68

Introduction...68

DIReCtional Troubleshooting Model.....................................70

Customer Interaction Skills Microcomputer Support
Case Scenarios–Part One...72

Customer Interaction Skills Microcomputer Support
Case Scenarios–Part Two...81

Customer Interaction Skills Microcomputer Support
Case Scenarios–Part Three 88

Customer Interaction Skills LAN Support
Case Scenarios...97

Customer Interaction Skills Network Interface Card
Case Scenarios..108

Customer Interaction Skills Wide Area Network
Support Case Scenarios 117

Customer Interaction Skills Internet Support
Case Scenarios..127

Customer Interaction Skills Macintosh Support
Case Scenarios..133

OBJECTIVES

At the completion of this chapter, you will be able to relate the steps of the DIReCtional troubleshooting model to various real-life scenarios.

INTRODUCTION

As a computer support professional, the sets of skills you bring to the job are activated when the phone rings or when you meet with a customer. To be effective, you must be very knowledgeable and have strong technical skills. You must also be able to apply the troubleshooting and communication skills presented in this book. The graphic below shows how the communication skills are interwoven into the DIReCtional model to illustrate the fact that both sets of skills are crucial.

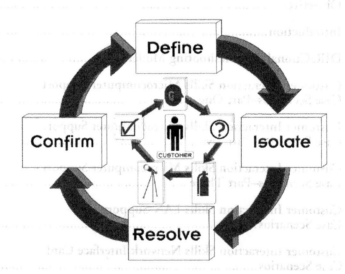

The purpose of this chapter is to put all of this knowledge to work. We have included a series of real-life case scenarios on the support of technologies in the Complete A+ Computer Support program. These case scenarios are in such areas as LANs, Network Interface Cards, the Internet, Windows 95, and PC hardware. They apply the technical, communications and troubleshooting skills that are presented in this program. Try them out and see how you do. Maybe the next call that you receive will be very similar to the situations you are about to encounter.

The case scenarios follow a similar disciplined format. The repetition is designed to help the problem diagnosis and resolution process become a natural reaction. The organizational and computing environments are presented from a "big picture" perspective for each topical area. A series of real-life based support scenarios are outlined for each "situation." The scenarios are presented within the methodical DIReCtional model process. The enclosed boxes represent the series of actions that fall within the procedural steps of Define, Isolate, Resolve, and Confirm. Interactive questions which encourage participant role play are identified by a number and letter combination. There are no right or wrong answers. However, suggested responses can be found in Appendix B.

As a refresher before the case scenarios, several job aids are included on the DIReCtional model and the hardware, software, and environmental conditions checklist.

Stop now and view the following video presentation on the Interactive Learning CD-ROM (Supplemental):

Customer Satisfaction

 Interactive Exercises

 Conclusion

DIRECTIONAL TROUBLESHOOTING MODEL

Step	In this step you will
1. Define the Problem	1. Describe the problem. 2. Determine the problem type. 3. Specify the conditions. 4. Try a quick fix. 5. Document everything pertaining to the problem. 6. Set expectations.
2. Isolate the Occurrence	1. Reproduce the problem. 2. Classify the problem. 3. Reconfirm the problem. 4. Document.
3. Resolve the Problem	1. Research the problem. 2. Identify potential causes. 3. Eliminate unlikely causes. 4. Solve the problem. 5. Repeat the solution. 6. Document the resolution.
4. Confirm the Resolution and Expectations	1. Review case history. 2. Confirm with your customer. 3. Communicate the solution. 4. Document final findings.

Hardware, Software, and Environmental Conditions Checklist

Check this	To verify
❑ **Hardware**	Exactly what equipment was your customer using? (Was she running an application on her computer with a networked or stand-alone printer?) • Processor (manufacturer, family, clock speed) • Addressable RAM memory • Usable hard-disk space • Video specifications (manufacturer, family, resolution) • Monitor specifications (manufacturer, size, resolution) • Add-ins. This includes additional drives, modems, application cards, etc. • Network interfaces (manufacturer, network type and version, configuration)
❑ **Software**	What programs are installed on your customer's system? Was she working in a Windows application? Did she have several programs open on her desktop? Did she toggle from a Windows application to a DOS application? Make certain to list all applications installed on your customer's computer such as: • Operating system (such as Windows NT) • Networking system (such as Novell v4.1) • User applications (MS Word, MS Office, Word Perfect, etc.) • Open applications
❑ **Environment**	Always indicate the physical environment surrounding the equipment. Was it in a clean, virtually dust-free surrounding (perhaps a laboratory), or in a cluttered office area? Checking the equipment's environment will go a long way in diagnosing the problem. List all conditions: • Connections • Clean/Dusty; Hot/Cold environment • Power source • Time of day

CUSTOMER INTERACTION SKILLS MICROCOMPUTER SUPPORT CASE SCENARIOS—PART ONE

The Situation

WZML is a small radio station. You provide computer support for the 10 employees who work at the radio station. Although there is a small network installed, most of the users work in a stand-alone mode running a Microsoft Windows user interface.

You receive five calls in quick succession one afternoon. All users sound urgent and cannot complete their work assignments until the problem is resolved.

1. What information is needed to fully Define the situation?
2. What potential situations need to be considered in order to Isolate the problem?
3. What action is required to Resolve the situation?
4. What follow up activity should be initiated to Confirm the situation?

The Calls

Call One

David calls to inform you that when his computer boots up, there are a couple of beeps and then nothing. His screen is black.

Call Two

Mary Ann has installed a new mouse on her system and it doesn't work. She would like you to fix this problem as soon as possible.

Call Three

Ever since Ralph moved to a different cubicle, his computer no longer works. He is complaining that he cannot get any work done without it.

Call Four

Bob leaves you a voice message. He is having problems with his PC. He states that his PC is "broken" and he thinks that he needs a new hard drive.

Call Five

Lois calls complaining that every time she turns on her computer, she gets a keyboard error. It just sits there and does nothing.

Call One

David calls to inform you that when his computer boots up, there are a couple of beeps and then nothing. His screen is black.

Define

1a. What can you ask David to help him better *describe* the problem?

....

....

1b. David confirms that the power cable is connected to the monitor. What can you have David try as a *quick fix*?

....

....

Isolate

1c. David double-checks the brightness and contrast dials are appropriately set. How would you ask David to *reproduce* the situation?

....

....

1d. What symptoms would you ask David to watch for in order to *classify* the problem as hardware or software?

....

....

Resolve

1e. David observes that during power up, neither the hard drive or floppy drive lights come on. He also doesn't hear the ticking associated with memory count up for which you asked him to listen. However, the computer LED power light is lit. What might you *identify* as a potential cause?

....

....

1f. You suspect the problem may be memory related. What steps would you take to *solve* the problem?

....

....

Confirm

1g. After walking over to David's work area, and verifying that you are properly grounded, you reseat the SIMMs. How would you *confirm* the problem has been resolved?

....

....

Review the problem and resolution with David. *Document* the trouble ticket.

Call Two

Mary Ann has installed a new mouse on her system and it doesn't work. She would like you to fix the problem as soon as possible.

Define

2a.   What questions would you ask Mary Ann to help *describe* the problem?

....

....

2b.   Mary Ann tells you that it is a PS/2 type of mouse. She checked the cable connection which is secure, and there are no error messages displayed. What other questions should you ask Mary Ann to *specify* the hardware and software conditions?

....

....

Isolate

2c.   Mary Ann tells you that she didn't install any software drivers. There was a diskette in the package, but since her old mouse worked fine, she didn't think she had to do anything except plug it in. What action should you take to *classify* the trouble as a software or hardware problem?

....

....

Resolve

Solve the problem with Mary Ann by talking her through the software driver load and Windows set up procedures. She reboots her system and her mouse is now operational.

Confirm

2d.   How would you confirm with Mary Ann that the problem has been resolved?

....

....

Mary Ann thanks you for your help. *Review* the problem and resolution with her, *communicating* the importance of software drivers to computer hardware components. *Document* the resolution of the problem.

Call Three

Ever since Ralph moved to a different cubicle, his computer no longer works.

Define

3a.   What questions could you ask Ralph to help determine the specific problem?

....

....

Isolate

3b.   Ralph tells you that the LED lights on the controller box are lit, and the attached printer initializes when he boots the PC. The monitor is blank. What questions would you ask Ralph to *classify* the problem as a monitor or video controller board problem?

....

....

Resolve

3c. Ralph checks the video cable and power cord connections which appear snug. What is your next step to eliminate any unlikely causes?

....

....

3d. At your request he removes the monitor cable from the back of the computer and examines the pins. Ralph asks if the pins are supposed to be bent, because three of them are. What steps would you take to *solve* the problem?

....

....

Confirm

3e. After walking over to Ralph's cubicle and carefully straightening the pins, reconnect the monitor cable. How would you *confirm* that the monitor is now working?

....

....

3f. What information should you *communicate* with Ralph to avoid future hardware problems?

....

....

Call Four

Bob leaves you a voice mail message. He is having problems with his PC. He tells you that he thinks it needs a new hard drive.

Define

4a. What questions can you ask Bob to more clearly *describe* the problems?

....

....

4b. Bob tells you that when he boots his machine nothing happens. What do you need to ask Bob in order to *specify* the hardware and software configuration?

....

....

Isolate

4c. Bob provides you the basic configuration information. What should Bob do to *reproduce* the problem?

....

....

4d. Bob reports that after booting the machine, "nothing happens." There are no display lights, noises, or images on the monitor screen. What actions would you take to further *classify* the problem?

....

....

Resolve

4e. Bob confirms that the computer power cables are properly connected. There is power to the wall outlet because his printer powers on. Bob remembers hearing an odd "whirring" sound for the past couple of weeks. What component do you *identify as a potential cause*?

....

....

4f. What must be done to further *research* the problem?

....

....

Document the status of the trouble ticket to date.

Confirm

Review the case status with Bob. *Communicate* your thoughts that the power supply needs to be replaced. Schedule a time with Bob when someone from your shop will be by to pick his computer up for service today and time estimate for the repair procedures to be completed within 24 hours of the equipment pick up.

Make a note to call Bob tomorrow afternoon to *confirm* that his computer is repaired.

Call Five

Lois calls complaining that when she turned on her computer this morning, the screen displays a keyboard error. The computer locks up and she can't get to any of her files.

Define

5a. On hearing the keyboard error, what *quick fix* would you suggest to solve the problem?

....

....

Isolate

5b. Lois checks the keyboard cable and pushes it more firmly into the keyboard interface port. What should she do to try to *reproduce* the problem?

....

....

Resolve

5c. Adjusting the keyboard cable appears to have *solved* the problem. What should Lois do to insure that she can *repeat* the situation?

....

....

Confirm

Review the problem resolution with Lois. *Confirm* her understanding of simple workstation triage techniques and *document* the trouble ticket.

CUSTOMER INTERACTION SKILLS MICROCOMPUTER SUPPORT CASE SCENARIOS—PART TWO

The Situation

The Iron Pipe and Fitting Company is a medium-sized manufacturing firm. You provide help desk support for the 35 microcomputer workstations. Recently, the computers were upgraded to Windows for Workgroups 3.11 and linked together using a peer-to-peer network configuration.

You receive four calls in quick succession one afternoon. All users sound urgent and cannot complete their work assignments until the problem is resolved.

1. What information is needed to fully Define the situation?

2. What potential situations need to be considered in order to Isolate the problem?

3. What action is required to Resolve the situation?

4. What follow up activity should be initiated to Confirm the situation?

The Calls

Call One

Bill calls to tell you that he cannot access the hard drive on his MS-DOS-based system.

Call Two

Linda is frantic. She tells you that her computer is broken and she needs to finish a critical report.

Call Three

Jason is having e-mail problems. He has an important text attachment in e-mail but cannot make changes on the attachment. He says that he is getting some "strange" error messages whenever he tries to save the file.

Call Four

Mary Jo leaves a message telling you that she is low on conventional memory and many of her applications will not run. She asks you to take a look at her computer to see if it is a serious problem or an easy fix.

Call One

Bill calls to tell you that he cannot access the hard drive on his MS-DOS based system.

Define

1a.   What can you ask Bill to better *describe* the problem?

   ....

   ....

1b.   Bill tells you that the problem started this morning and he gets no response when he tries to boot his machine. What questions should you ask Bill in order to *specify* the environmental conditions that might affect a microcomputer.

   ....

   ....

1c.   Bill relates that his work area is a standard cubicle office environment. What action should Bill initiate in order to help *determine* the problem type?

   ....

   ....

Isolate

1d.   Bill doesn't have a boot diskette, so you bring your master boot diskette to his workstation. At this point, you think there is a problem in the hard drive. What action should you take to *reconfirm* your suspicions?

....

....

Resolve

1e.   His workstation can boot from the floppy disk. When you try to access the C: Drive, you get an error message "Error Reading Drive C:". What steps can you take to *solve* the problem?

....

....

Confirm

Review the problem situation with Bill. You need to *communicate* the hard drive replacement process, explaining that tech support will try to restore the data from the drive, but unless there is a recent backup of the data, you can't be sure how much can be restored. *Confirm* Bill understands the scope of the situation.

Before *documenting* the trouble ticket, make a note to have someone *review* backup procedures with Bill when the new hard drive is installed and the computer is returned to him.

Call Two

Linda is frantic. She tells you that her computer is broken and she needs to finish a critical report.

Define

2a.   What questions can you ask Linda to better *describe* the problem?

....

....

2b.   Linda responds with a tirade about "stupid computers that make her job harder, not easier!" What can you say to calm her and gain a better understanding of the problem?

....

....

Isolate

2c.   Linda relaxes and explains that when she boots her machine it starts up as usual and then stops in the middle of the process. What should you ask her to do to *reproduce* the problem?

....

....

Resolve

2d.   Linda describes the messages that flash across the screen as her computer boots. The final error message reads, "Non-system disk or disk error. Replace and strike any key when ready." What would you suggest Linda do to *resolve* the problem situation?

....

....

Confirm

After Linda removes the floppy disk from the A: Drive, *review* the boot procedure priorities with her. *Confirm* that she understands the reason why the system wouldn't boot, and *document* the trouble ticket.

Call Three

Jason is having e-mail problems. He has an important text attachment in e-mail, but cannot make changes on the attachment. He says that he is getting some "strange" error messages whenever he tries to save the file.

Define

3a.   What type of information is required to *specify* the software configuration parameters of Jason's workstation?

....

....

3b.   What are some questions that you should ask Jason to *determine* the problem type?

....

....

3c.   What might you say to Jason *to set* his expectations regarding the possibility of opening the document?

....

....

Isolate

3d. Jason understands the possibilities and is willing to work with you to learn how to fix the problem file. What steps should Jason take to *classify* the specific software problem?

....

....

Resolve

3e. Jason *reproduces* the problem when he tries to save it to his document directory. How would you *research* this symptom in order to *identify* a potential problem cause?

....

....

3f. On reviewing the file attributes, you realize that the file is marked read-only. How can Jason easily *solve* this problem?

....

....

After changing the file attribute assignments using the Attrib command, Jason *repeats* the file save process and successfully completes the transaction.

Confirm

Confirm with Jason that he understands the file attribute procedures and *document* the trouble ticket.

Call Four

Mary Jo leaves a message telling you that she is low on conventional memory and many of her applications will not run. She asks you to take a look at her computer to see if it is a serious problem or an easy fix.

Define

4a.   What questions can you ask to *determine* the specific problem type?

....

....

4b.   Mary Jo tells you that she constantly is receiving an "Out Of Memory" error message. What information needs to be *specified* in order to better understand the hardware and software configurations?

....

....

Isolate

4c.   In order to *reconfirm* the problem is memory related, what DOS command should you ask Mary Jo to invoke in order to identify current memory usage?

....

....

Resolve

4d.   After running the **MEM** command, Mary Jo tells you that her machine has 385 KB of conventional memory, and 150 KB of upper memory free. How would you suggest that Mary Jo further *research* the memory utilization?

....

....

After issuing the **MEM /C** command, Mary Jo reads you the list of files that are using conventional memory. You realize that all of the TSR programs are using conventional memory and not loading into upper memory. Mary Jo can *solve* her problem by running MEMMAKER which will optimize her conventional memory usage by shifting some of the existing programs from conventional memory into upper memory.

Confirm

Confirm Mary Jo understands the basic parameters of memory management. *Review* the functions of the MEM and MEMMAKER utilities that Mary Jo can use as a daily tool. *Document* the problem resolution.

CUSTOMER INTERACTION SKILLS MICROCOMPUTER SUPPORT CASE SCENARIOS—PART THREE

The Situation

Wright Architecture and Design is a medium-sized architectural firm that recently upgraded its computer systems from a Windows 3.11 environment to a Microsoft Windows NT platform. You provide end user computer support for the new Microsoft Windows NT Workstation 4.0 users.

You receive five calls over the course of the morning. All five users are frantic because they do not understand the new operating system and need to complete their assignments now.

1.   What information is needed to fully Define the situation?

2.   What potential situations need to be considered in order to Isolate the problem?

3.   What action is required to Resolve the situation?

4.   What follow up activity should be initiated to Confirm the situation?

The Calls

Call One

Charles calls; he is frantic because he cannot log into his Windows NT Workstation and has forgotten the Administrator password on the machine.

Call Two

Tony received a new printer to attach to his Windows NT Workstation. He plugged it in, but it is still not working.

Call Three

Debbie installed a new 2.0-GB hard drive in her desktop computer. She wants to partition and format the drive as an NTFS volume. She is wondering if she should use FDISK to prepare the hard disk for use.

Call Four

Mickey moved a file from his Windows NT Workstation to a shared drive on Charles' Windows NT Workstation. Now he cannot edit the file.

Call Five

Olive is trying to view the Security log on her Windows NT Workstation, but is receiving an "Access is Denied" message.

Call One

Charles calls; he is frantic because he cannot log into his Windows NT Workstation and has forgotten the Administrator password on the machine.

Define

1a.   What is the first question that you might ask to *determine the problem type*?

....

....

Isolate

1b.   Charles tells you that he is logged into a local workstation. What additional questions might help you *classify the problem*?

....

....

1c.   Charles is sure that he typed everything correctly and wants you to give him back his old system that "worked." What can you do to *reproduce* the problem?

....

....

Resolve

1d.   Charles discovers that his Caps Lock was on when he was typing the password. What can Charles do to *solve the problem*?

....

....

Confirm

1e.   Charles turns off the Caps Lock and successfully logs onto the system. *Review* the problem with Charles, reminding him that NT Workstation is case sensitive. *Document* the trouble ticket.

Call Two

Tony received a new printer to attach to his Windows NT Workstation. He plugged it in, but it is still not working.

Define

2a.   What can you ask Tony in order to *specify the environmental conditions* related to the printer connection?

....

....

2b.   Tony tells you that he unpacked the printer, attached the parallel cable to the back of his computer, and plugged the printer into the power outlet. What procedures should you ask Tony to complete in order to try a *quick fix*?

....

....

Isolate

2c.   Tony verifies that all the cable connections are firmly attached and the power light is turned on. What should you ask Tony to *classify* the situation as a software problem?

....

....

Resolve

2d.   Tony did not initiate the Add Printer Wizard. What can Tony do to *solve the problem*?

....

....

Confirm

2e.   After completing the Wizard, Tony thanks you for your help. How can you *confirm* that the problem was resolved?

....

....

Document the trouble ticket.

Call Three

Debbie installed a new 2.0-GB hard drive in her desktop computer. She wants to partition and format the drive as an NTFS volume. She is wondering if she should use FDISK to prepare the hard disk for use.

Define

3a.   Before Debbie initiates any action, what additional information do you need to *specify the conditions*?

....

....

Isolate

3b.   Debbie tells you that this drive is a second drive. The primary drive is formatted with FAT. What are some important questions to ask Debbie in order to *reconfirm* the workstation configuration?

....

....

Resolve

3c.   Debbie's workstation recognizes the drive as the second drive. No files have been loaded on to the drive, so it is blank. Once you *identify potential problem causes*, how would you recommend Debbie to proceed to format the drive as an NTFS volume?

....

....

Confirm

3d.   After walking Debbie through the formatting procedures, how would you *confirm* that her system is properly recognizing the new NTFS partition?

....

....

Review the process with Debbie. *Document* the trouble ticket.

Call Four

Mickey moved a file from his Windows NT Workstation to a shared drive on Charles' Windows NT Workstation. Now he cannot edit the file.

Define

4a.   What questions would you ask Mickey to *determine the problem type?*

....

....

4b.   Mickey doesn't know whether he is using an NTFS or FAT file system. How can you determine which file system they are using to *specify the operating environment?*

....

....

Isolate

4c.   Mickey tells you that the properties screen lists NTFS as the assigned file system. Ask Mickey to *reproduce* the problem by moving another file to the shared directory.

....

....

4d.   Mickey tells you that the same problem occurs with the second file. What question should you ask Mickey to better *classify* the situation as a system or individual problem?

....

....

Resolve

4e. Mickey and Charles sit in the same work area. What is the next logical step to *research* the problem?

....

....

4f. Charles is able to edit the file in the shared directory. What action needs to be taken to *solve* the problem and provide Mickey editing capabilities?

....

....

Confirm

4g. Charles assigns Mickey the permissions necessary to edit files on the shared directory. How can Mickey *confirm* that the problem is resolved?

....

....

4h. *Review* the need to have permissions in the destination directory when moving files in an NTFS environment with both Mickey and *document* the trouble ticket.

....

....

4i. How might you *broadcast* this tip to all users who might share files?

....

....

Call Five

Olive is trying to view the Security log on her Windows NT Workstation, but is receiving an "Access is Denied" message.

Define

5a. What should you ask Olive as a *quick fix*?

....

....

Isolate

5b. Olive doesn't know which groups her login is assigned. Where can you direct her to *reconfirm* her group memberships?

....

....

Resolve

5c. Olive is a member of the Users and Power Users groups. *Identify* the problem is based on the fact that she is not assigned rights to the Security log because she is not a member of the Administrators or Domain Admins local group.

Confirm

5d. *Review* Olive's group assignments with her. What action can you suggest she take in order to gain access to the System log?

....

....

5e. *Document* the trouble ticket. *Communicate* the situation to the primary system administrator to alert them to Olive's request.

CUSTOMER INTERACTION SKILLS LAN SUPPORT CASE SCENARIOS

The Situation

The Brandywine Company has decided to upgrade its centralized mainframe computer system to take advantage of some of the benefits of the newer local area network technologies. Specifically, it wants to offer each department the autonomy to determine the best information processing procedures for the local units, while ensuring accurate data using a centralized database. Other features that Brandywine was looking forward to were electronic mail, remote telecommuting access, fax server capabilities, and other types of resource sharing. The mainframe will continue to be maintained in order to support several mission-critical applications. Three departments that work with front-line, high-profile, high-security mission-critical programs will not transition to microcomputers during the initial project implementation phase.

This normal IT scenario presents a series of challenges. Because the implementation is planned as a phased project, the technical support staff will need to fully support both systems. In addition to managing shared resources such as the fax server and printers, technical support staff will also need to provide support to remote telecommuters. Several tiers of password protection will augment the well-defined file security.

Five calls come into the technical support hotline in quick succession one Monday morning. All users sound urgent and cannot complete their work assignments until the problem is resolved.

1. What information is needed to fully Define the situation?
2. What potential situations need to be considered in order to Isolate the problem?
3. What action is required to Resolve the situation?
4. What follow up activity should be initiated to Confirm the situation?

The Calls

Call One

Fred cannot access the inventory management program which is a mission-critical application.

Call Two

Cory must deliver a disaster recovery plan before noon today, and cannot access a building maintenance database file that is vital.

Call Three

Martha cannot access the fax server in order to get a product spec sheet to a client who wants to make a purchase decision today.

Call Four

Blake, one of the staff managers piloting the telecommuting program, reports that odd characters are appearing in the middle of a corporate presentation that is due before the end of the day.

Call Five

Steve has sent a file to the shared printer three times, but cannot get the document to print.

Call One

Fred cannot access the inventory management program which is a mission-critical application.

Define

1a. Ask Fred to describe his workstation. Is it a mainframe-type or a microcomputer? If he doesn't know, what questions could you ask him to help him *describe* his computing environment?

....

....

1b. Fred identifies his workstation as one of the newly installed microcomputers. What other information is needed to *specify* the problem conditions? (Hint: where is the problem located: microcomputer, gateway hardware, or mainframe?)

....

....

Isolate

1c.   Fred tells you that it is his first day without a training coach. The system worked last Friday, but won't come up today. What questions do you need to ask to *classify* the problem as a single user or system-wide problem?

....

....

Fred tells you that everyone else's workstations are operational. In lieu of any definitive information, you ask him to *reproduce* the problem by walking through his startup procedure from a cold boot start. Fred's user login and password combination does not give access to the file server. Fred remembers that his trainer always logged him on to the system.

Resolve

1d.   *Research* the user administration records to verify Fred's user login activation. Fred's name is not in the user records. The network administrator must add Fred to the network. What is your next course of action to *solve* the problem?

....

....

Confirm

Review Fred's problem with the network administrator. *Communicate* any required activity and time frames back to Fred or his supervisor. *Document* the support call. Make a note to call Fred to *confirm* that his login has been activated and all other services are functional.

Call Two

Cory must deliver a disaster recovery plan before noon today, and cannot access a building maintenance database file that is vital.

Define

2a.   What questions would you ask Cory to better *describe* the problem situation?

....

....

2b.   Cory tells you that he has never had a problem gaining access to the maintenance database which is on the mainframe. He just follows the prompts and keys in the file directory information. This time he received an error message and was locked out of the file. What would you ask him to *determine* if the problem is known or unknown?

....

....

2c.   Cory tells you that the error message reads "error 15-f, no file found." What might you suggest Cory try as an *immediate solution*?

....

....

Isolate

2d.   *Reproduce* the problem situation by walking Cory through the maintenance database access procedures. Cory is able to successfully access the mainframe database. What could you ask Cory to *reconfirm* your understanding of the original problem conditions?

....

....

2e.   *Reconfirm* any differences in the procedures or workstation configuration.

....

....

Resolve

2f.   Why would you ask Cory to *repeat* the solution by exiting the application (without rebooting), entering the application he was using prior to the initial problem, and reinitiating a request for access to the mainframe database?

....

....

Confirm

Confirm the problem is resolved with no specific cause identified and *document* the trouble ticket.

Call Three

Martha cannot access the fax server in order to get a product spec sheet to a client who wants to make a purchase decision today.

Define

3a. What would you ask Martha to *determine* if the problem is operational user error or system based?

....

....

Martha tells you that this is the first time that she has used the fax server, but she has always wanted to try it, and this account was a great opportunity. You ask Martha to *describe* the procedures that she tried. Martha followed the appropriate menu-driven procedures. You try an *immediate solution* by walking her through a series of DOS prompt commands. Access is still denied.

Isolate

3b. What can you do to *reproduce* the problem?

....

....

You try to access the fax server from your workstation and are successful. *Reconfirm* the problem with Martha. You tell her that you will research a resolution and get back to her with an answer as quickly as possible.

Resolve

3c. What resources can you check to *identify* the potential causes for Martha's limited access to the fax server?

....

....

After checking Martha's resource assignments and user profile, you learn that she has not yet been given access to the fax server.

Confirm

3d. *Document* the trouble ticket and initiate *communications* to the network administration group by filling out the required change request forms. You discover that a higher level of authorization is required to enable user access to the fax server resource. How would you *communicate* the resolution procedures and estimated time frames to Martha?

....

....

3e. Martha is not pleased that she cannot use the fax server application immediately. She does not understand why she was not assigned privileges, or why if you know the resolution, you can't implement it. She becomes increasingly irate and does not want to wait for standard operating procedures. How would you constructively respond to Martha?

....

....

When the network administration group notifies you that Martha's privileges have been expanded, call Martha to *confirm* the completion of services. *Document* the closed trouble ticket.

Call Four

Blake, one of the staff managers who is piloting the telecommuting program, reports that odd characters are appearing in the middle of the corporate presentation that is due before the end of the day.

Define

4a. What questions would you ask Blake to better *describe* the problem situation?

....

....

4b. Blake tells you that she sometimes receives an odd character in her transmission when there are thunderstorms, but never this consistently. What questions might you ask her to *determine* if the problem can be traced to a known situation?

....

....

4c. Blake tells you that she accessed her mail files early this morning, but she has only noticed the odd characters when she was downloading the large graphics files. None of the rest of the text files seem to be affected. What questions would you ask her to *specify* the conditions of the remote communications environment?

....

....

4d. Blake verbally reviews the hardware and software configurations that match your organization's standard configuration specifications. What would you say to Blake to *set her expectations* regarding a quick solution?

....

....

Isolate

4e. Blake cannot stay on the line any longer to work with you to *classify* the problem as intermittent or duplicateable. How would you respond to her need to resolve the situation, but inability to participate in the resolution?

....

....

4f. What do you need to know in order to try to *duplicate* the conditions and reproduce the problem?

....

....

Resolve

4g. *Research* the problem by checking the options on all the modems of the internal modem pool against Blake's modem set up configuration. The options all appear to be compatible, but you remember seeing an e-mail message regarding new drivers available from the modem vendor and think the new driver might *eliminate* a potential problem cause. What is your next course of action?

....

....

Confirm

4h.   Call Blake to *review* the case history of the trouble. *Communicate* the fact that you were unable to duplicate the problem, but that you were in touch with the manufacturer and will download the most recent driver update. *Confirm* Blake knows how to load the new driver. If Blake sounds hesitant, what advice would you offer her?

....

....

Document the trouble ticket and *communicate* the location of the new driver through your organization's information channels.

Call Five

Steve has sent a file to the shared printer three times, but cannot get the document to print.

Define

5a.   What questions would you ask Steve in order to *determine* if the trouble is located at the printer or within the print server software?

....

....

Steve tells you that he was able to print earlier today, and agrees to walk over to check the printer status in order to *specify* the physical conditions.

Isolate

Steve reports that the LCD display shows an error code 45 which *classifies* the situation as an identifiable problem.

Resolve

5b. *Research* the error code 45 in the printer manual, which *identifies* the potential problem cause as a paper jam. How would you work with Steve to *solve* the problem?

....

....

Confirm

After the jam is clear, *confirm* with Steve that the printer is back online and operational. *Document* the trouble incident.

CUSTOMER INTERACTION SKILLS NETWORK INTERFACE CARD CASE SCENARIOS

The Situation

The Trumble Trucking Company expanded operations, bringing on several new employees in each department. A variety of new Pentium microcomputers have been purchased. You have been recruited to help install the new machines and to load the basic application modules.

The microcomputers arrived with the hardware fully configured from the manufacturer, but several machines cannot connect to the network when you tried to install them. How would you respond to each of following situations? Make sure that you address each of the four points listed below.

1. What information is needed to fully Define the situation?

2. What potential situations need to be considered in order to Isolate the problem?

3. What action is required to Resolve the situation?

4. What follow up activity should be initiated to Confirm the situation?

The Calls

Call One

One machine passes all of the POST tests during boot up, but it cannot attach to the network.

Call Two

Several machines display an error message that no physical connection can be made to the network.

Call Three

Two machines are able to connect to the network after the initial software configuration. However, once they are rebooted, no network connection can be made. The technicians have reinstalled the machines three times.

Call Four

Several ISA cards with plug and play capabilities were ordered to upgrade network access performance of the in place 486 machines. When they are installed, the 486 machines running Windows v3.1 no longer can see the network.

Call One

One machine passes all of the POST tests during boot up, but it cannot attach to the network.

Define

1a.   What would you do to *determine* if the problem is local to the machine or related to the network?

....

....

1b.   The error message says "server not found" and your installation boot diskette does not achieve connectivity. What is the first *quick fix* to try?

....

....

1c.   If reinserting the network interface card (NIC) does not provide a connection, what would you do to better *specify* the environmental conditions?

....

....

Isolate

1d.   After verifying that the I/O interrupt and DMA memory assignments meet the standard configurations defined by the Trumble organization, what would you do to *classify* the situation as a duplicateable problem?

....

....

When placed in another new machine, the NIC *reproduces* the problem situation. However, when placed in an older microcomputer, the NIC proves operational.

Resolve

1e.   Can you *identify potential causes* that might cause this sporadic problem?

....

....

1f.   What sources might you use to *research* a possible solution?

....

....

1g.   After *researching* the NIC manufacturer's home page, you realize that two different NIC card versions were received. The slightly earlier release had difficulty working with some microcomputer hardware BIOS; however, a patch was made to the original driver. Downloading the patch from the home page will *solve* the incompatibility problem. What should you do to verify the *quality control* of this solution?

....

....

Confirm

1h. After *documenting* the patch and NIC card revision numbers, what is your next course of action to *communicate* the new patch fix to the rest of Trumble's internal support group?

....

....

1i. How would you *confirm* that this was the appropriate fix to the incompatibility problem?

....

....

Call Two

Several Pentium machines display an error message that no physical connection can be made to the network.

Define

2a. What is your first course of action to *specify the conditions* in order to better understand the problem?

....

....

2b. On inspection, you realize that the network adapter card is one of the new Plug and Play (PnP) interface card types. You remember that Pentium motherboards have a PnP activation switch. What type of *quick fix* might you try?

....

....

Isolate

2c.   You locate the PnP switch and place it in the "on" position. What would you do to try to *reproduce* the problem?

....

....

Resolve

2d.   The machine boots up and connects to the network. What is your next step to *repeat* the problem and validate the solution for *quality control*?

....

....

Confirm

2e.   *Review and document* all of the variables affecting the installation of this type of PnP card. How would you communicate this information to your internal support staff for future reference?

....

....

Call Three

Two of the Pentium machines are able to connect to the network after the initial software configuration. However, once they are rebooted, no network connection can be made. The technicians have reinstalled the software three times.

Define

3a. What questions can you ask the installation technicians to better *describe* the reboot procedures?

....

....

3b. The technicians tell you, "CMOS settings are only lost when the microcomputers are powered off." What questions would you ask them to *determine* if the problem is software or hardware?

....

....

Isolate

3c. What action can you take to further *classify* the problem as an isolated incident or defective hardware?

....

....

3d. How would you *reproduce the problem*?

....

....

Resolve

3e. When the cards are inserted into an older 486 machine, the software settings remain constant during the power off/power on sequence. When a NIC card with a single interface connection is installed in one of the questionable Pentium machines, the software settings remain constant after powering off. What is your next step to *research the problem*?

    ....

    ....

3f. Your visual review of the NIC card does not reveal any manually adjustable jumpers. What can you do to *identify potential problem causes*?

    ....

    ....

3g. The installation guide doesn't offer any suggestions or explanations. What other alternative sources can you use *to research*?

    ....

    ....

3h. The NIC card manufacturer's customer service telephone hotline was busy when you tried to dial. On searching their Web site for recent software patches, you discover that several other clients had sent help requests that appeared very similar to yours. The technical support response suggested there might be a problem with the motherboard BIOS software. What is your next step to *eliminate potential causes*?

    ....

    ....

3i. Searching the Pentium manufacturer's Web site, you discover that there have been several revision patches for the BIOS software for your model. After downloading the most recent patch and installing the patch in the first machine, the problem appears to be *solved*, what should you do to *quality assure* the solution?

....

....

Confirm

3j. *Review* your notes of the trouble scenario and document a consolidated history. How do you *communicate* the resolution to the rest of your organization's support team so that they will be able reference this type of problem in the future?

....

....

3k. Is there anyway to *confirm* that the BIOS patch is a permanent fix for those Pentium machines?

....

....

CUSTOMER INTERACTION SKILLS WIDE AREA NETWORK SUPPORT CASE SCENARIOS

The Situation

The Caldecott Company is headquartered in Omaha, NE. Five regional locations are located across the United States in Boston, Cleveland, Memphis, Houston, and Sacramento. Field sales reps and technical support staff work remotely out of their homes or hotel rooms so that they can maintain close customer ties. Each of the field personnel dials into the nearest regional hub information system via a 14.4-Kbps modem, where it is relayed to headquarters or another regional office via the nationwide frame relay network.

Currently, the sales reps access regional pricing and inventory information directly from the regional hubs, where the information is maintained. Engineering specifications, corporate-wide sales and inventory information are maintained at the corporate office. All field personnel access their electronic mail from their assigned regional hub.

1. What service access points are involved?

2. What information is needed to fully Define the situation?

3. What potential situations need to be considered in order to Isolate the problem?

4. What action is required to Resolve the situation?

5. What follow up activity should be initiated to Confirm the situation?

The Calls

Call One

Jim, the Phoenix sales rep, calls because he can't access the regional hub to update a sales quote. He called an inside sales rep to get the answer quickly, but he needs access when he is on the road during off hours.

Call Two

Sally, the Atlanta technical field rep, has an ISDN connection from her home, but is having difficulty accessing some engineering specifications from the central computer.

Call Three

The Memphis office is having difficulty transmitting end-of-quarter sales numbers to headquarters. Ralph, the sales vice-president's administrative assistant, calls you to find out why his boss can't make his deadline.

The Caldecott Corporation Wide Area Network

Diagram the national network including the three remote locations specified in the above help desk scenarios.

Call One

Jim, the Phoenix sales rep, calls because he can't access the regional hub to update a sales quote. He called an inside sales rep to get the answer quickly, but he needs access when he is on the road during off hours.

Configuration Diagram

Diagram the wide area network configuration that links Jim to the Caldecott network. Identify the access points that link the geographic locations.

Define

1a.   What would you ask Jim to *determine* if this is an operational or system problem?

....

....

1b.   Jim tells you that he has been using the system to get sales quotes for several months since the system was installed. What would you ask him in order to better *specify* the remote transmission environment?

....

....

1c.   Jim tells you that he just upgraded his modem to a 28.8-Kbps model. What would you ask him in order to further *specify* the environmental conditions?

....

....

Jim tells you that he does not hear any dial tone when he dials out using the communications program. Try a *quick fix* by asking Jim to reassign the COM port.

Isolate

1d.   Ask Jim to reproduce the situation by:

....

....

Resolve

Jim tells you the problem is *solved*, and *repeats* the procedure one more time.

Confirm

Document Jim's call and add a brief note to your weekly reminder check list to *communicate* to all remote users the importance of reviewing the COM port assignment when installing new modems.

Call Two

Sally, the Atlanta technical field rep, has an ISDN connection from her home, but she is having difficulty accessing some engineering specifications from the central computer.

Configuration Diagram

Diagram the wide area network configuration that links Sally to the Caldecott network. Identify the access points that link the geographic locations.

Define

2a. What would you ask Sally in order to *describe* the communication break down?

....

....

2b. From Sally's description, it sounds as if the problem is in the link between the regional hub and corporate headquarters. What would you ask her to further *specify* the environmental conditions?

....

....

2c. Sally's ability to access e-mail helps you to *determine* the problem area. What is your next course of action? How will you *set her expectations* for a problem solution?

....

....

Isolate

Reproduce the problem by trying to access the frame relay network from your workstation. You are not allowed access.

Resolve

2d. What network components can you *identify* as potential causes?

....

....

Research the problem by calling the regional hub internetwork administrator who monitors the local routers. He checks the router that provides access to the frame relay network and sees that it was never brought back on-line after the weekend's diagnostic routines. He *solves* the problem by rebooting the router. What do you do to *repeat* the scenario to verify the resolution is the correct one to resolve the connection problem?

Confirm

2e. *Review* the case history and *document* the incident. What is your next course of action to *confirm* the solution with your client, Sally?

....

....

2f. How might you suggest *communicating* the incident with the rest of the internal support staff to remind folks that all maintenance procedures need to be completed?

....

....

Call Three

The Memphis office is having difficulty transmitting end of quarter sales numbers to headquarters. Ralph, the sales vice-president's administrative assistant, calls you to find out why his boss can't make his deadline.

Configuration Diagram

Diagram the wide area network configuration that links Ralph to the Caldecott network. Identify the access points that link the geographic locations.

Define

3a. What questions would you ask Ralph to better *describe* the situation?

....

....

3b. Ralph tells you that there is an error message, "resources not available." What is your next series of questions to *determine* if the problem can be identified as the regional hub or at the headquarters end of the connection?

....

....

3c. Ralph can access electronic mail and the regional sales files. What other questions might you ask to further *specify* the environmental conditions and better define the problem?

....

....

3d. From your discussion with Ralph, you are sure that the problem is not operational, but somewhere in the network system components. How should you *set* Ralph's (and those of his boss) expectations?

....

....

Isolate

3e.   What is your next step to *classify* the problem as an intermittent or ongoing problem?

....

....

You try to access the corporate network from your workstation, but your attempt is unsuccessful. Therefore, you must escalate the trouble ticket to the regional network systems staff.

Resolve

The regional network systems engineer at your location *researches* the diagnostics on the local frame relay router. All local systems test positive. He will call his liaison contact at headquarters to further *identify* potential causes.

He calls you back with the news that the headquarter's LAN is down. They hope to *solve* the problem within the hour.

Confirm

3f.   Although the problem is not fully resolved, what is your next course of action to *communicate* the current status of the trouble report back to your client, Ralph, and the rest of the support team?

....

....

3g.   What information would you *document* to maintain current information?

....

....

3h.   When you get the news that the headquarter's LAN is operational, what should you do to *confirm* the news?

....

....

CUSTOMER INTERACTION SKILLS INTERNET SUPPORT CASE SCENARIOS

The Situation

The Brandywine Company of Portland, ME, successfully implemented the new local area network. Several departments experimented with Internet access. The vice-president for Human Resources wants to incorporate some of the point and click features of the Internet and create an easy-to-use interface for all employees to access employee benefits and records. He has heard that an intranet will enable the employees in the regional offices in Colorado Springs and San Antonio to access confidential records with the same level as employees in the Portland headquarters.

The phased implementation of Intranet connectivity will be integrated into the current Microsoft Windows 95 network. The centralized help desk personnel located at the Portland headquarters will provide troubleshooting services for the wide area linkages.

During the first week of the Intranet implementation, you receive several calls. Most of them sound very urgent.

1. What information is needed to fully Define the situation?

2. What potential situations need to be considered in order to Isolate the problem?

3. What action is required to Resolve the situation?

4. What follow up activity should be initiated to Confirm the situation?

The Calls

Call One

Helen, who is located in the Colorado Springs office, tried to access the Internet to find a Home Page that relates to small business. When she clicks on her Internet icon, no connection is initiated.

Call Two

Scott called to tell you that his Internet e-mail did not work.

Call Three

Kris called and said she can't find a file that she downloaded from an FTP site, which is needed to update a PC application. She needs the patch to complete a report that must be delivered before the end of the day.

Call One

Helen, who is located in the Colorado Springs office, tried to access the Internet to find a Home Page that relates to small business. When she clicks on her Internet icon, no connection is initiated.

Define

1a.   What questions could you ask Helen so that she can better *describe* the situation?

....

....

1b.   Helen tells you that she has been able to access the Internet all week since it was installed, but this afternoon she began receiving "can't start application" messages. What would you ask her to help *specify* the hardware and software conditions of her workstation?

....

....

Apparently, Joe updated her Inventory Management application this morning. Helen doesn't think he changed anything else on her machine. You tell Helen that you will check with Joe and *set her expectations* that you hope to get her a quick resolution.

Isolate

Classify the problem as intermittent or duplicateable by trying to access the Internet from your workstation.

Resolve

1c. You successfully access a Web page which leads you to *identify* the Inventory Management application upgrade as a potential cause of Helen's problem. What would you do next to further *research* a solution?

....

....

1d. *Eliminate potential causes* by asking Joe if the application patch might have changed workstation configuration. Joe says he didn't change anything. He only added the IP address for the new update. Which configuration files could possibly have been updated?

....

....

Joe tells you that he didn't verify the settings of any of the .INI files. You ask Joe where he found the IP address that he used for the update. Joe tells you that he made it up. In order to solve Helen's problem, the original IP address needs to be assigned to the application configuration file. Joe promises to return to Helen's desk today to change the IP address assignment at her workstation.

Confirm

Call Helen to *review* the necessary application configuration changes and to let her know that Joe will fix her workstation before the end of the day. *Document* the solution on the trouble ticket. *Communicate* via e-mail to all technical support group members reminding them about the appropriate IP address assignment procedures. Make a note to remember to call Helen to *confirm* that she regained Internet access.

Call Two

Scott called to tell you that his Internet e-mail did not work.

Define

2a. What questions would you ask Scott to describe what exactly is not working?

....

....

Isolate

2b. Scott tells you that he was checking his mail when he tried to open a message, but only garbage characters was displayed. What information is needed to *classify* the problem as intermittent or duplicateable?

....

....

Resolve

2c. Scott opens several messages and reads you a summary of the contents. The fifth message that he opened was garbled. You think there may be a conflict with the encoding parameters. Where can you *research* the configuration parameters assigned to Scott's workstation?

....

....

2d. Scott tells you that the MIME button is not checked. Instruct Scott to activate the MIME button to *solve* his data format problem. What actions need to be initiated to *repeat* the situation in order to verify the resolution is correct.

....

....

Confirm

Scott *confirms* he can read both formerly garbled messages. *Review* the encoding parameters with Scott for future reference. *Document* the trouble ticket.

Call Three

Kris called and said she can't find a file that she downloaded from an FTP site, which is needed to update a PC application. She needs the patch to complete a report that must be delivered before the end of the day

Define

3a. What questions should you ask Kris in order to *specify* the environmental conditions of her workstation?

....

....

Isolate

3b. Kris tells you that she is connected to the LAN, but she always saves her files to her C: Drive. What should you do to *reproduce* the situation to determine the location of the lost file?

....

....

3c. Kris gets very irate that you would infer that she is not capable of transferring a file. There is a virus on the network and you should use your time to find and destroy it, instead of having her go through these ridiculous exercises! How would you respond to Kris?

....

....

Kris walks through the FTP transfer process very slowly, *reproducing* each step while you are on the line. Kris notices that the save location is automatically assigned to a different drive than her desktop workstation. She admits to not thinking that the default save location would be anywhere, except her local C: Drive.

3d. What is the next step that Kris should take to *reconfirm* the default location?

....

....

Resolve

3e. How would you *solve* Kris' problem and transfer the patch to the application program located on the C: Drive of her workstation?

....

....

Confirm

3f. *Review* the problem with resolution with Kris and confirm that she understands the default drive assignment. *Document* the trouble ticket. How can you *communicate* this problem and its resolution to other Internet/intranet users?

....

....

CUSTOMER INTERACTION SKILLS MACINTOSH SUPPORT CASE SCENARIOS

The Situation

The Paintbrush Graphics Company is a commercial art studio. Fifty Macintosh computers are linked together via an Appletalk network.

You receive four calls in quick succession one morning. All users sound urgent and cannot complete their work assignments until the problem is resolved.

1. What information is needed to fully Define the situation?

2. What potential situations need to be considered in order to Isolate the problem?

3. What action is required to Resolve the situation?

4. What follow up activity should be initiated to Confirm the situation?

The Calls

Call One

Jennifer is having problems booting her PowerPC. Do you have time to come by and look at it?

Call Two

Sam is having problems printing to a network printer. He is getting error messages that the printer cannot be found, but other people are printing

Call Three

Herschel has a Macintosh icon on his monitor that looks very sad. He cannot do anything with his system.

Call Four

Carol has a bomb on her monitor that says "Sorry, a System Error Has Occurred." She does not know what to do.

Call One

Jennifer is having problems booting her PowerPC. Do you have time to come by and look at it?

Define

1a. What questions can you ask Jennifer to better *describe* the problem?

....

....

1b. Jennifer tells you that there have been no configuration changes and she doesn't remember an error message. What questions should you ask Jennifer to *specify* the hardware and software configurations?

....

....

Isolate

1c. What can you ask Jennifer to do to *reproduce* the problem?

....

....

Resolve

1d.   Jennifer suddenly remembers that she installed a new utility package. What potential situations can you *identify* as a potential cause?

....

....

1e.   You believe the problem may be due to an extension conflict. What actions can Jennifer initiate to *eliminate* potential conflicts?

....

....

Confirm

After completing the trial and error process, you identify the offending extension. *Confirm* that Jennifer's computer is operational. *Review* the impact that conflicting extensions have on the Macintosh. *Document* the trouble ticket. Make a note to *communicate* the impact of conflicting extensions in next month's tips and tricks user newsletter.

Call Two

Sam is having problems printing to a network printer. He is getting error messages that the printer cannot be found, but other people are printing.

Define

2a.   What questions can you ask Sam to *determine* the specific problem?

....

....

Isolate

2b.   What questions can you ask Sam to classify the problem as printer or application related?

....

....

Resolve

2c.   It appears that everyone can print to the printer except Sam, although he is connected to the network. What actions should Sam pursue to *identify* some potential problem causes.

....

....

2d.   Sam is not familiar with the Chooser. How can you help him *research* the problem?

....

....

After opening Chooser, Sam saw that there was no printer assigned. He *solved* the problem by selecting the appropriate LaserWriter printer.

Confirm

2e.   What action should Sam take to *confirm* the solution is appropriate?

....

....

Confirm Sam understands the function of the Chooser utility and *document* the problem.

Call Three

Herschel has a Macintosh icon on his monitor that looks very sad. He cannot do anything with his system.

Define

3a.   What questions can you ask Herschel to help *determine* the problem type?

....

....

3b.   What action can you suggest Herschel to try as a *quick fix*?

....

....

Isolate

3c.   The Mac will not boot, even with the *SHIFT* key depressed, which eliminates the possibility of an extension conflict. How would you *classify* the problem?

....

....

Resolve

3d.   What *potential causes* can you identify as the problem?

....

....

3e.   What actions can Sam initiate to *eliminate* unlikely causes?

....

....

3f.   Booting from the Disk Tools floppy diskette and zapping the PRAM does not fix the problem. What could you try next?

....

....

After opening the case and reseating all boards and chips, the Macintosh starts up correctly and the problem is *solved*.

Confirm

3g.   While *reviewing* the case history with Herschel, he wonders if the SIMM chips and boards could have jarred loose when the Mac fell off his desk yesterday? How should you react to Herschel's new information?

....

....

Communicate the necessity of telling technical support of any non-standard incident. These help define which troubleshooting procedures to pursue. *Document* the trouble ticket.

Call Four

Carol has a bomb on her monitor that says "Sorry, a System Error Has Occurred." She does not know what to do.

Define

4a.   What questions can you ask Carol to *determine* the problem type?

....

....

4b.   Carol tells you that she was installing a shareware games program when the problem occurred. What action can you suggest Carol try as a *quick fix*?

....

....

Isolate

4c.   Carol's Mac restarted without any problem. What action should Carol initiate to *reconfirm* the problem?

....

....

Resolve

4d.   When Carol restarts the game application, the Macintosh displays a System Bomb message #26. You *research* the specific error message and find that it indicates a Bad Launch Program. What steps should you take to *solve* the problem?

....

....

Confirm

After Carol removes the games package, all of the standard supported applications on her Mac are able to open without incident. *Review* the case history with her. *Communicate* the destructive nature of unsupported shareware applications which can be incompatible, cause an extension conflict, or even contain a virus. *Document* the trouble ticket.

Appendix A—Answers to Pre-Test and Post-Test Questions

CHAPTER 1

Pre-Test Answers

1. Dependence on service industries for economic growth

2. It costs five times more to gain a new customer than to retain an existing customer.

3. Technical, Troubleshooting, Communications

Post-Test Answers

1. Preventive maintenance and end-user training

2. Your Customers

3. How

4. Choose from any of the following:

   A. Being called back when promised

   B. Receiving an explanation on how a problem happened

   C. Knowing who to contact with a problem

   D. Being contacted promptly when a problem is resolved

   E. Being allowed to talk to someone in authority

   F. Being told how long it will take to resolve a problem

   G. Being given useful alternatives if a problem can't be solved

   H. Being treated like a person, not an account number

   I. Being told about ways to prevent a future problem

   J. Being given progress reports if a problem can't be solved immediately

5. Communication skills

CHAPTER 2

Pre-Test Answers

1. Telephone Help Desk, Field Service Organizations, Depot Service

2. The following items are suggested answers.

    A. Balancing administrative requirements and customer urgency

    B. Identifying escalation strategies

    C. Maintaining customer documentation

    D. Maintaining an orderly work area

    E. Observing copyright infringement policies

3. Customer records enable you to track trends that can identify problems and promote preventive maintenance strategies.

Post-Test Answers

1. Suggested answers include:

    Telephone help desks receive incoming calls from a distributed user population. Problem diagnosis is usually completed remotely or escalated to a field service technician.

    Field service organizations provide face-to-face troubleshooting support at the customer's equipment location.

    Depot service provides equipment repair functions at a central location. Customers deliver equipment to the depot repair site.

2. The following are suggested answers:

    A. How does your client define a major service outage?

    B. What resources are available to assist with service recovery?

    C. What are the decision points for escalation?

    D. Who is the primary decision-making contact?

    E. Are there parallel backup systems available?

3. Review the documentation in your customer file.

4. The following are suggested answers:

    A. The top ten problems and associated resolutions

    B. Escalation procedures and contact phone numbers

    C. Vendor contact information

    D. Unresolved intermittent problems and possible fixes

5. No

CHAPTER 3

Pre-Test Answers

1. Define, Isolate, Resolve, and Confirm

2. Suggested answers include client records, supplier information, and bulletin boards, third-party reference books, professional peers, and the Internet.

3. Confirm with the client that the problem is fully resolved.
   Broadcast innovative solutions to your colleagues.
   Document resolution in customer record.

Post-Test Answers

1. Who, what, when, where, why, and how

2. Equipment and software configurations

3. The following are suggested answers:

    A. Check the connectors.

    B. Check all power switches.

    C. Check system resources.

    D. Check available memory.

    E. Check new hardware or software installation.

4. Documentation

5. Monthly newsletters, Internet FAQ lists, Group e-mails

CHAPTER 4

Pre-Test Answers

1. Listening, questioning, handling difficult situations, setting expectations, following up
2. Eye contact, positive body language, note taking
3. Remain calm.

Post-Test Answers

1. Careful listening will help you gain information that will help you solve the problem, as well as exhibiting respect for your customer's situation.
2. Ask for clarification, summarize your customer's comments, and confirm your understanding of the situation.
3. "C" designates a closed question. "O" designates an open question.

    C   Which directory did you assign as a default?

    O   Why did you choose this particular setup configuration?

    C   What was the displayed error code?

    C   Can you describe what other applications were open?

4. Acknowledge, Listen, Empathize, Respond, Thank
5. Establish a working partnership.

    Promise only what you can deliver.

    Set realistic resolution time frames.

    Document commitments and dates.
6. If the customer is not comfortable with the resolution, the problem is not fixed.

Appendix B — Case Scenarios

OVERVIEW

There are no necessarily right or wrong answers to the Case Scenarios within Chapter 5. The following are suggested questions and procedures to respond to the customer help desk situation.

CUSTOMER INTERACTION SKILLS MICROCOMPUTER SUPPORT CASE SCENARIOS—PART ONE

Call One

1a. Is the monitor power cord firmly connected to the power source?

Are any status lights lit on the monitor?

Has any new hardware or software been installed recently?

1b. Verify the brightness and contrast dials are set properly.

1c. Ask David to reboot the computer.

1d. Ask David to watch the status LEDs for the hard drive and floppy drives to verify system accessibility. Also, he should listen for any beep tones.

1e. A memory problem because memory is counted before the drives are accessed.

1f. Walk over to David's work area, verify you are properly grounded, open the casing, and reset the SIMM chips.

1g. Ask David to reboot the computer and verify that it is functioning properly.

Call Two

2a. Are there any error messages?

What type of mouse did you install?

Is the mouse cable firmly connected?

2b. What mouse drivers are you using?

What software application are you running?

Is your software application mouse compatible?

2c. Walk Mary Ann through the mouse driver install procedures, including the Windows Setup procedures.

2d. Ask Mary Ann to reboot the system and open the application to verify the mouse is working.

Call Three

3a. What is the computer doing differently that makes you say "it no longer works?" Did you change the hardware configuration when you moved? Could the any of the components been dropped during the move?

3b. Verify that the monitor power cable is firmly plugged into a live outlet. Verify the monitor cable is firmly attached the CPU unit.

3c. Ask Ralph to unplug the video cable to the monitor and examine the physical pins.

3d. Walk over to Ralph's cubicle and carefully straighten the pins and reconnect the monitor.

3e. Power up the PC and verify that the monitor is properly displaying computer activity.

3f. Remind Ralph that computer cable terminator pins are very sensitive. When ever he disconnects or connects a cable, great care should be taken not to bend or break them.

Call Four

4a. What specific problems are you noticing?

Why does he think he needs a new hard drive?

4b. What is the computer manufacturer and model number?

What operating system and applications is it running?

4c. Ask Bob to reboot the computer while you are on the phone and report any error messages, status light activity, or beep sounds.

4d. Ask Bob to check the power cords and power source to verify power is being sent to the computer.

4e. The power supply

4f. The problem resolution seems to be to replace the power supply. However, the PC is under warranty and you would like to have the maintenance company run some more extensive diagnostics.

Call Five

5a. Ask Lois to check her keyboard connection to verify that it is firmly attached.

5b. Reboot the computer and report to you any error messages or beep tones.

5c. Verify that Lois can issue several keyboard commands. Reboot the system and confirm the ability to issue keyboard commands.

CUSTOMER INTERACTION SKILLS MICROCOMPUTER SUPPORT CASE SCENARIOS—PART TWO

Call One

1a. What error messages are displayed?

Did he notice any recent occurrence that might have been a warning symptom?

1b. What are the environmental conditions in his area?

Is there any continually operational electronically powered equipment nearby?

Are you near any open windows?

1c. Ask Bill if he can boot from his A: Drive using a system diskette.

1d. Reboot the machine from the floppy in the A: Drive.

1e. The problem is definitely related to a hard drive failure. The hard drive will need to be replaced. Check with Bill to see if a data backup procedure was recently run to assist with data restoration, otherwise, data retrieval from the failed hard drive will need to be run.

Call Two

2a. Does the computer boot up?

Are the status lights lit on the monitor and CPU?

What beeps do you hear when the computer is turned on?

2b. Explain that you understand how frustrating it is when things you expect to work break. Let her know that if she will work with you, you are sure that the problem can be found relatively easily. Her computer should be operational shortly.

2c. Reboot her system and watch for any error messages or beep tones during the start up process.

2d. Remove the floppy disk in the A: Drive.

Call Three

3a. What e-mail program is he using?

3b. What is the error message that is displayed when he tries to save the file?

3c. There are a couple of options that might successfully open the file, but you can't make a firm promise.

3d. Ask Jason to save the file again while you are on the line.

3e. Walk Jason through the DOS Attrib command procedures to verify the file attributes.

3f. Help Jason remove the read-only attribute using the command-line prompts or GUI-based utility.

Call Four

4a. Ask Mary Jo why she thinks she has a memory problem.

4b. What applications are you running?

Which applications will not run?

What operating system are you using?

4c. The **MEM** command.

4d. Reissue the **MEM** command using the /C parameter to identify which files reside in conventional memory.

CUSTOMER INTERACTION SKILLS MICROCOMPUTER SUPPORT CASE SCENARIOS—PART THREE

Call One

1a. Are you trying to login into a local workstation or a domain?

1b. Did you recently change your password?

Are you sure you are using the proper case to type your password?

1c. Ask Charles to retype the password slowly to make sure there wasn't an accidental typing mistake.

1d. Turn the Caps Lock off.

Call Two

2a. Are the printer status lights lit?

Is the power strip turned on?

2b. Are the cables firmly attached to the printer and the PC?

2c. Have you run the Add Printer Wizard?

2d. Walk Tony through the Add Printer Wizard.

2e. Ask Tony to print a test page.

Call Three

3a.   Is this a bootable hard drive or an additional drive?

3b. Are there any files located on this drive?

Does Windows NT recongize the second drive as being installed?

3c. Ask Debbie to log in as the Administrator and walk her through the Disk Administrator procedures.

3d. Ask Debbie to open Explorer and try copying files from her C: drive to her new drive.

Call Four

4a. Is the file system NTFS or FAT?

4b. Assist Mickey in checking the directory properties in My Computer or the Explorer.

4d. Are any other co-workers having problems editing files?

4e. Ask Mickey to check with Charles to see if he can edit the file.

4f. Charles needs to assign Mickey permissions to the shared directory.

4g. Ask Mickey to edit the file.

4i. E-mail broadcast or help desk newsletter

Call Five

5a. Which local groups are you assigned?

5b. Walk Olive through the steps to access her account using the User Manager.

5d. She can call or e-mail the system administrator to adjust her group membership assignment.

CUSTOMER INTERACTION SKILLS LAN SUPPORT CASE SCENARIOS

Call One

1a. Has your workstation recently been replaced?

Is the cable that connects your workstation into the wall a modular wall plug?

Does your workstation have a CPU box attached to it?

1b. Can your workstation power on?

What applications or features can you access?

Is there an error message on your machine?

1c. Can any one else in your group access the Inventory Management program?

1d. Call the network administrator to verify if they have the new employee paperwork to add Fred to the system.

Call Two

2a. When was the last time you used the building maintenance database?

Have you ever had this problem before?

Has anyone made any changes to your software or hardware configuration?

Is there an error message on your screen?

2b. Ask him to read you the error message.

2c. Reboot his workstation.

2d. Were any of these procedures different from the ones you used earlier when you were denied access?

2e. Ask Cory to repeat any steps that might have been different.

2f. To verify that a batch or executable file was not rewriting the Inventory Management batch commands.

Call Three

3a. Have you been able to access the fax server previously?

Did you receive an error message? What did it say?

3b. Access the fax server from your workstation to verify that the server is working.

3c. Check access privileges assigned to Martha's login.

3d. Call Martha and explain that the fax server was installed for specific marketing projects and that to ensure its availability, access is limited to those with supervisor approval. She needs to have her supervisor initiate the paperwork.

3e. One option is to simply listen to Martha, empathize, and review the reasons for the policy. Another option, if possible, is to assist her by sending the information to this single important client today while the paperwork is being processed.

Call Four

4a. What do these characters look like?

Are your transmissions interrupted by these characters often?

Are there machines, such as a washing machine or air conditioner fan nearby?

Have you tried terminating the faulty connection and initiating a new call?

4b. Have these characters appeared in any other applications that you were using today?

4c. At what speed are you transporting data?

What brand of modem are you using?

Are the status lights in their normal mode, or is one of them a different color or state from normal?

Let's review the port settings of your communications package.

4d. You tell her the hardware and software configuration looks standard, but if she wants you can work with her to try a couple of different options.

4e. You will check the record logs to see how many other people are having this problem There must be something going on with the phone lines. However, you will try to duplicate the situation and if you find anything, you will call her back.

4f. The phone number and applications she was accessing remotely.

4g. Initiate a search on the modem manufacturer's Web site.

4h. If she can access the Internet while you are both speaking, offer to walk her through the process. Otherwise, offer her step-by-step instructions.

Call Five

5a.   Were you able to print any documents today?

If yes, were you printing from a different application?

If no, can anyone else in your general area print?

Offer to verify default printer assignments.

5b.   Talk Steve through the proper method to open the printer case and remove the jammed paper.

CUSTOMER INTERACTION SKILLS NETWORK INTERFACE CARD CASE SCENARIOS

Call One

1a.   Taking the path of least resistance, try to boot from a known master boot diskette. Try to connect another machine.

1b.   Double-check cable connections.

Reinsert network interface card.

Reboot the workstation.

1c.   Verify and document the I/O interrupt and DMA memory assignments, double-checking for any memory conflicts.

1d.   Install the malfunctioning NIC in another machine.

Install a working NIC into the "broken" machine.

1e.   Different BIOS versions might cause incompatibility.

1f.   The manufacturer's documentation that came with NIC and/or the Internet are good research sources.

1g.   Install the new software driver patch on the incompatible systems, boot, and connect to the network.

1h.   There are several options. Your choice will depend on your organization's procedures. Some suggestions are:

Send an e-mail.

Post a notice on the FAQ list.

Publish a note in the monthly tech newsletter.

1i.   Maintain a record of all problems during this phase of the implementation. Track how many BIOS incompatibilities occur and how many are fixed using the downloaded patch.

Call Two

2a.   Double-check the NIC card is compatible with the newer Pentium processor.

2b.   Activate the PnP switch on the Pentium motherboard.

2c.   Reboot the machine and try to attach to the network.

2d.   Check the motherboards of the other Pentium machines and activate dormant PnP switches.

2e.   Send a message via e-mail.

Post a note on the FAQ board.

Verbally tell as many people as you can find.

Call Three

3a.   Does any particular system information appear to change when the systems are rebooted?

Did you check the CMOS settings after the software installation and then after the system was rebooted?

Do the cards all have the same interface connection settings?

3b.   Are the hardware and software configurations of these two machines any different from the configurations of the new machines that are working normally?

3c.   Change out a hardware component.

3d.   Install the NIC card in another machine.

Install a known, working NIC card in the machine in question.

3e.   Install the working NIC card in the other non-working machines, to try to repeat the result.

3f.   Refer to the NIC manufacturer's information for potential incompatibility warnings.

3g.   Call the NIC manufacturer's hot line or Web page.

3h.   Search the Pentium vendor's Web page.

3i.   Install the patch on the other machines and attach them to the network.

3j.   Communicate via an e-mail broadcast.

Post a message on the FAQ list.

Make an announcement at the next group meeting.

3k.   Reboot the machines several times to insure the CMOS remains stable.
Place an entry in the Pentium workstation's repair file and try to flag any future problems.

CUSTOMER INTERACTION SKILLS WIDE AREA NETWORK SUPPORT CASE SCENARIOS

Call One

1a. When you dial to get any kind of dial tone sound?

Describe the procedure that you used to try to gain access to the regional computer.

1b. Did you make any modifications to your hardware or software configuration recently?

1c. Ask Jim to review the set up parameters in his communications program.

1d. Dialing into the regional hub computer

Call Two

2a. Are you able to access any part of the corporate computer network?

Describe the procedures you followed to try to access the central computer.

2b. Can you access the inventory and e-mail applications?

2c. Tell Sally that it looks as if the problem is between the regional hub and corporate headquarters. You need to contact the technicians who manage the wide area links. You hope to call her back shortly with a solution, but you can't make any promises until you understand the situation.

2d. The router between the two computing hubs, the communications lines, the modems, or the remote LAN

2e. Call Sally to let her know that the problem was at the headquarters link end, but the situation is resolved and she should be able to dial into the central computer.

2f. Send a broadcast e-mail to the support team.

Place an entry in the FAQ list.

Call Three

3a. Can anyone in the Memphis office link to the headquarters computer?

Did you receive any error messages?

3b. Ask Ralph if he can access his e-mail and the regional pricing spreadsheet.

3c. Describe the procedures that you are using to access the computer.

3d. Tell Ralph that the problem requires a little more research and you do not have an immediate answer, but will notify him as soon as you can identify a resolution.

3e. Try to access the corporate network from your workstation.

3f. Call Ralph and let him know that the problem is on the remote end. Relay the information that the trouble should be fixed in approximately one hour. You understand the urgency of the situation and will keep him posted. Notify the rest of the staff verbally, via e-mail, or a system-wide message regarding the status of the Corporate LAN.

3g. Update the trouble ticket with the information at hand, keep it open until Ralph is back "online."

3h. Call Ralph as quickly as possible, and then forward the information to the rest of the support staff.

CUSTOMER INTERACTION SKILLS INTERNET SUPPORT CASE SCENARIOS

Call One

1a. What error message appears on the screen?

How long have you been accessing the Internet?

When was the last time that you accessed the Internet?

What procedure did you follow to try to connect?

1b. What changes were made to your workstation's software or hardware configuration recently?

Was anyone else using your workstation today?

1c. Call Joe to review the Inventory Management application upgrade procedures.

1d. WIN.INI, SYSTEM.INI, or PROTOCOL.INI

Call Two

2a. Can you open your e-mail application?

Are you able to send and receive mail?

Describe exactly what features or functions you feel are broken.

2b. Have you received this type of garbled message previously?
Are all of your messages garbled, or just a few?

2c. Check the message format properties of the mail icon under the Control Panel in Windows 95.

2d. Restart the machine, retrieve, and open the mail messages.

Call Three

3a.   Are you connected to a network, or dialing out as a stand-alone machine?

3b.   Ask Kris to repeat the ftp transfer step-by-step while you are on the line.

3c.   Explain the virus might be a possibility, but it is always best to begin troubleshooting by eliminating certain possibilities. You have found a methodical approach which checks off each item helps to speed the problem diagnosis process. You know her time is valuable, and you appreciate Kris working with you to resolve the problem quickly and efficiently.

3d.   Identify the designated default drive. Perform a simple directory search to confirm it did download to the virtual directory location.

3e.   Copy the patch from the network drive to Kris' C: Drive.

      Redirect the ftp file save parameter to the correct drive location.

3f.   Send a broadcast e-mail to all Internet users.

      Post a note on the FAQ list.

      Write a brief article in the monthly users tips and tricks newsletter.

CUSTOMER INTERACTION SKILLS MACINTOSH SUPPORT CASE SCENARIOS

Call One

1a.   Have you made any recent software or hardware changes to your Mac configuration?

      Has an accidental situation like a liquid spill affected your workstation?

1b.   What model PowerPC are you using?

      What version of Mac OS is installed?

1c.   Restart the Mac, documenting any error messages and listening for any signal-type sounds.

1d.   Possible extension conflict, software installation could have deleted required system files, or hardware failure

1e.   Restart Mac with *SHIFT* key depressed to disable extensions. Move all extensions into a temporary file. Move each extension, one at a time, into the System folder, and restart machine, until extension conflict is identified.

Call Two

2a. Were you able to print from the network printer earlier today? Any time previously?

2b. Can any other people in your group print from the designated printer?

Are you attached to the network?

Is the printer turned on?

2c. Review the Chooser assignments.

2d. Walk Sam through the process of opening Chooser and selecting the appropriate printer assignment.

2e. Print a document.

Call Three

3a. What peripherals are connected to the Mac?

Did he recently install any new hardware or software packages?

3b. Restart Mac with the *SHIFT* key depressed to disable extensions.

3c. Most likely a hardware problem, possibly software.

3d. Possibly a problem with the hard drive, a PRAM or SIMM.

3e. Ask Sam to find his Disk Tools floppy and reboot the system from the utility disk. Sam should then try deleting PRAM.

3f. Open the case and verify the SIMMS and other internal components are firmly seated.

3g. The fact that the Mac was dropped is very important information for the troubleshooting process. Accidents happen, but we wasted valuable time checking for software errors when we could have quickly resolved the problem.

In the future, don't be afraid to be honest, the trouble will get fixed faster.

Call Four

4a. What programs were you running when the system error occurred?

Did you recently make any changes to the hardware or software configurations?

4b. Restart the Mac from a cold boot.

4c. Restart the games application.

4d. Remove the shareware program.

Index

A

ALERT! 56

C

Case History 28, 42
Closed-Ended Questioning 54
Conditions 28, 32, 71
Confirm the Resolution and
    Expectations 28, 42, 70
Copyright Limitations 22
Core Competencies 11
Customer 8, 18-20, 22,
    27, 29, 35, 57-58, 61
Customer Interaction Skills 11
Customer Service Organization 17

D

Define the Problem 28-29, 70
Depot Service 20
Difficult Situations 56
DIReCtional Model 27
DIReCtional Troubleshooting 20, 25, 27
DIReCtional Troubleshooting
    Model 42, 70
Document 28, 37-38, 42, 44, 59
Documentation 21, 31, 34
Documenting Problem Resolutions 62
Duplicateable Problem 37

E

Escalation 22
Escalation Policy 21
Expectations 28, 35, 42, 58
External Resources 39

F

Face-to-Face Techniques 50
Field Service 19
Following up 60
Frequently Asked Questions
    (FAQ) 31, 39, 63

H

Help Desk 7, 18
Help Desk Challenges 20

I

Intermittent Problem 22, 37
Internal Resources 38
Internet Technical Resources 40
Isolate the Occurrence 28, 70
Isolate the Problem 36

L

Listening Techniques 50

O

Open Service Calls 43
Open-Ended Questioning 53
Organizational Structure 18

P

Problem Type 31

Q

Questioning Skills 53
Quick Fix 28, 33

R

Resolve the Problem 28, 38, 70

S

Service Expectations 9
Suggestions 62

T

Telephone Techniques 52
Troubleshooting Reference
    Library 31, 38, 44

V

Video
    Communication Skills 17
    Conclusion 69
    Customer-Centered Service 8
    Interactive Exercises 69
    Overview 8
    Troubleshooting 28